Swords or Ploughshares?
The Morgenthau Plan
for Defeated
Nazi Germany,
1943-1946

Warren F. Kimball

Rutgers University, Newark College

The America's Alternatives Series

Edited by Harold M. Hyman

Swords or Ploughshares?

The Morgenthau Plan for Defeated Nazi Germany, 1943-1946

J. B. Lippincott Company
Philadelphia/New York/San Jose/Toronto

ISBN 0-397-47350-8
Library of Congress Catalog Card Number 75-33057
Printed in the United States of America

1 3 5 7 9 8 6 4 2

Library of Congress Cataloging in Publication Data

Kimball, Warren F.
    Swords or ploughshares?

    (The America's alternatives series)
    Bibliography: p. 167
    1. Reconstruction (1939-1951)—Germany. 2. Germany—History—Allied occupation, 1945- . 3. Reconstruction (1939-1951)—Germany—Sources. 4. Germany—History—Allied occupation, 1945- —Sources. I. Title. II. Title: The Morgenthau plan for defeated Nazi Germany, 1943-1946.
D829.G3K53   940.53'144'0943   75-33057
ISBN 0-397-47350-8

For PAULA, TOM, and DONNA

Contents

Foreword

"When you judge decisions, you have to judge them in the light of what there was available to do it," noted Secretary of State George C. Marshall to the Senate Committees on the Armed Services and Foreign Relations in May 1951.[1] In this spirit, each volume in the "America's Alternatives" series examines the past for insights which History—perhaps only History—is peculiarly fitted to offer. In each volume the author seeks to learn why decision-makers in crucial public policy or, more rarely, private choice situations adopted a course and rejected others. Within this context of choices, the author may ask what influence then-existing expert opinion, administrative structures, and budgetary factors exerted in shaping decisions: What weights did constitutions or traditions have? What did men hope for or fear? On what information did they base their decisions? Once a decision was made, how was the decision-maker able to enforce it? What attitudes prevailed toward nationality, race, region, religion, or sex, and how did these attitudes modify results?

We freely ask such questions of the events of our time. This "America's Alternatives" volume transfers appropriate versions of such queries to the past.

In examining those elements that were a part of a crucial historical decision, the author has refrained from making judgments based upon attitudes, information, or values that were not current at the time the decision was made. Instead, as much as possible he or she has explored the past in terms of data and prejudices known to persons contemporary to the event.

1. U.S., Senate, Hearings Before the Committees on the Armed Services and the Foreign Relations of the United States, *The Military Situation in the Far East*, 82d Cong., 2d sess., part 1, p. 382. Professor Ernest R. May's "Alternatives" volume directed me to this source and quotation.

Nevertheless, the following reconstruction of one of America's major alternative choices speaks implicitly and frequently, explicitly to present concerns.

In form, this volume consists of a narrative and analytical historical essay (Part One), within which the author has identified by use of headnotes (i.e., Alternative 1, etc.) the choices which he believes were actually before the decision makers with whom he is concerned.

Part Two of this volume contains, in whole or part, the most appropriate source documents that illustrate the Part One Alternatives. The Part Two Documents and Part One essay are keyed for convenient learning use (i.e., the references in Part One will direct readers to appropriate Part Two Documents). The volume's Part Three offers the user further guidance in the form of a Bibliographic Essay.

Vietnam triggered many sharp debates, especially on university campuses, among students of American diplomacy's ends and means. Critics who attended particularly to the development and implementation of United States foreign policy since 1941, have become increasingly skeptical about the purity of this nation's purposes and methods. One of the pivotal points in this ongoing argument is the policy which America evolved during World War II toward the enemy powers, especially Nazi Germany.

Consequences of enduring impact in our lives, and of great magnitude globally, stem from that policy. Thirty years have passed since the events Professor Kimball describes and analyzes in this volume. But readers in the Bicentennial decade need to know accurately the paths that our past heads of state decided to travel, and to avoid, else distortions of history creep too easily into considerations about future alternatives. Professor Kimball's scrupulous, un-shrill review of the Morgenthau Plan, one of the major options concerning Hitler's Reich available to America's policy-makers of World War II, is particularly meaningful today.

Harold M. Hyman
Rice University

Preface

Alternatives are present whenever major policy decisions are made, and identifying those alternatives as the decision-makers perceived them is an enlightening process. One quickly finds that alternatives which are once rejected often reappear, slightly disguised, again and again. What seems to be a clear decision to select one plan of action over another is frequently modified or even reversed at a later date. Equally confusing is the continued life of an alternative within the enormous and labyrinthian American governmental bureaucracy, even after being publicly dismissed by presidents and cabinet officers.

What appears on the surface to have been the impulsive acceptance by Churchill and Roosevelt of the Morgenthau Plan for the pastoralization and reform of Germany was actually the culmination of an intensive and wide-ranging debate within the American government. The repudiation, a few weeks later, of that same plan, similarly turns out to be far more complicated than a mere response to public opinion—the interpretation given the change by most historians. Paul Hammon has argued that the bureaucrats in the War Department triumphed on the question of postwar planning for Germany, while Anthony Kubek has bitterly condemned the Treasury Department bureaucracy for exercising an unconstitutional degree of control over American foreign policy. Bruce Kuklick and Gabriel Kolko have argued the same thing, though from slightly differing perspectives, for the liberal-capitalists within the Department of State. Certainly the actions of individual leaders can be understood only within the context of the choices presented to them, and those options are understandable only within the context of the society and bureaucracy which spawned them. Nevertheless, Franklin D. Roosevelt made decisions (or procrastinated such decisions) in ways which frequently frustrated the bureaucracy. In spite of steady pressure from the State Department, he refused to adopt a "get tough" policy toward the

Soviet Union; nor did he ever waver from his belief that all Germans, not just the Nazis, were guilty of aggression and crimes against humanity even though the bulk of the State and War department staffs took the opposite position. Ultimately, the liberal-capitalism of the State Department won out, but not until after Roosevelt's death.

This study proceeds from my long-term research into the foreign policy of President Franklin D. Roosevelt. The American Council of Learned Societies, the American Philosophical Soceity, and the Research Council of Rutgers University have provided essential and extensive assistance for that research, and I am most grateful for their support. Ploughing through the documents has been made more pleasurable by the invariably courteous and wise assistance of the staffs at the Franklin D. Roosevelt Library, the State Department Archives at the National Archives, and the Public Record Office in London, England (in spite of what a more suspicious person might think was a British and/or United States Postal Service conspiracy to lose documents).

The series editor, Harold Hyman, has been remarkably patient and perceptive. It has been a privilege to be associated with him. I must also acknowledge an intellectual debt to Gabriel Kolko and Anthony Kubek; for it was my reading of their totally contradictory and disparate analyses of the Morgenthau Plan for Germany which initially stimulated my interest. Those who labor out of friendship deserve special thanks. With their names usually buried in a brief preface (such as this), such unselfish scholars make indispensable contributions to our craft. Charles C. Alexander of Ohio University and Herbert P. Meritt of the Newark College of Rutgers University read the entire manuscript and added enormously to whatever style and logic it possesses. Lloyd C. Gardner of Rutgers College cheerfully acted as a sounding board for all sorts of my hare-brained ideas, often managing to make me confront my contradictions. My already great debt to J. Joseph Huthmacher of the University of Delaware is only increased because of his contribution. Most of all I thank my wife, Jacqueline, for without her this would still lie buried in my notes and in my mind.

Warren F. Kimball
Rutgers University, Newark College

Part One

Swords or Ploughshares?

1

Introduction: Thoughts on Postwar Germany, 1941-1944

On September 15, 1944, President Franklin D. Roosevelt and British Prime Minister Winston S. Churchill, meeting at the Historic Citadel in Quebec, Canada, initialed a memorandum which indicated their agreement on what came to be known as the Morgenthau Plan for Germany. The key sentence in the brief statement seemed clear and unambiguous:

> This programme for eliminating the war-making industries in the Ruhr and in the Saar is looking forward to converting Germany into a country primarily agricultural and pastoral in its character (see Document 1).

The six priorities for such a reordering of Germany's economic and social structure were outlined in only four sentences. Initially came the goal of full *disarmament*. The two leaders reasoned that since heavy industry could always be converted easily to arms production, only *deindustrialization* could effectively prevent the rebirth of German war-making capabilities. Next the note recalled the devestation visited upon Russia and the Allies and concluded that much of the industry in the Ruhr and the Saar could be removed as *reparations* to replace those losses. Finally, the paper called for the governance of the Ruhr and the Saar by a world organization then under consideration; in other words, the *dismemberment* of Germany. It was against that backdrop that Churchill and Roosevelt saw the picture of a Germany "primarily agricultural and pastoral in its character"; it is that last phrase which envisages two extensive social changes in Germany, *denazification* and *demilitarization*. A "pastoral" state, with all the overtones of peaceful, bucolic farmers which those words bring to mind, could hardly support a modern military establishment or provide nourishment for the militant, aggressive nationalism long associated with Prussia and Germany.

With remarkable conciseness, this memorandum captured the essential elements of the debate over the postwar future of Germany. Only the issue of zonal boundaries did not appear, and that was largely a function of geography and the questions of reparations and dismemberment. Winston Churchill dictated the actual memo. With his characteristic economy of words, the prime minister managed to join together the many issues which British and American planners had treated largely as separate, unrelated issues. As is so often true of a decision made at the very top, Churchill and Roosevelt gave no precise instructions as to the way in which their goals were to be implemented. Nor did they clarify some of the more ambiguous phrases. For example, the dismantling of industry referred specifically only to the Saar and Ruhr, the heart but not the whole of German industrial facilities. Yet the conversion of Germany into a pastoral nation implied the elimination of heavy industry from the entire nation.

More important than such vague instructions was the context within which the policy statement appeared. Roosevelt had consistently refused to make firm decisions about postwar Germany. As a result, no single department or organization within the American governmental bureaucracy could take control over such planning. Instead, the two offices most obviously concerned—the State Department and the War Department—each developed its own program for its own reasons. In the face of indecision, the Treasury Department, initially interested only because of the problems of occupation currency and monetary support for a postwar German currency, eventually seized the initiative by offering a comprehensive plan which took advantage not only of Treasury Secretary Henry Morgenthau's special personal relationship with the president, but also capitalized on the general anti-German atmosphere which understandably permeated official Washington.

The Alternatives

Even before the 1944 Quebec meeting, four broad schemes for the postwar role of Germany had appeared. All of them overlapped in some of their details, but each was philosophically different.

Alternative 1: the Morgenthau Plan. Embodied in the Roosevelt-Churchill memorandum signed at Quebec, this plan aimed at psychological and social reform by destroying Germany both as a state and as an industrial power. Morgenthau and his advisors argued that the only sure means of eliminating German aggression were to demolish Germany's military and industrial capabilities and to remake the German character—with the first contributing to the success of the second.

Alternative 2: the War Department plan. This plan, developed primarily by various army organizations concerned with the problems of administering the immediate postwar occupation of Germany, dealt largely with short-term questions, though the answers often had long-term ramifications. The army remained primarily concerned with eliminating civilian interference during the occupation and avoiding political or economic responsibilities. Occupied more with law and order, efficiency, and maintaining the traditional American separation between military and political planning which had characterized wartime thinking, army planners for postwar Germany addressed themselves primarily to administrative structure and organizational problems within the military chain of command, rather than to questions of long-term economic reconstruction or dismemberment. Nonetheless, the army's concern for efficiency quickly translated into such proposals as that suggesting the use of prewar and wartime German bureaucrats as administrators and the immediate conversion of German industry to peacetime production, which went against the spirit and the letter of the Morgenthau Plan. Even so, the War Department found an ally in Morgenthau when it opposed the primacy of political planning over all else. At least initially, both saw the State Department's plan to reconstruct German industry, even with adequate safeguards, as a negation of the purpose of the war. Although army planning gave no indication of any desire for a vengeful peace, military men had no inclination to simply let bygones be bygones.

Alternative 3: the State Department's plan. This approach represented Secretary of State Cordell Hull's thinking as well as that of most of the career foreign service officers. A bulwark of Wilsonian thought, the Department of State roundly condemned the "unjust" and "punitive" aspects of the Treaty of Versailles for having prodded Germany into accepting Hitler and his policy of war to redress the injustice of the peace. They were determined not to make that mistake again. In addition, Hull's simplistic economic theories were generally in accord with the sophisticated political economy sought by the department. Hull and his advisors firmly believed that an economically sound and self-supporting Germany was essnetial to the economic rehabilitation of Western Europe and that America's prosperity depended heavily upon recovery in Europe. Hull and the State Department were not immune to the prevailing hatred for Nazi Germany; in fact, the Secretary of State initially supported Morgenthau's concept of a punitive peace. But the department was more concerned with long-term issues. Convinced that world peace could come only when economic crises and jealousies had been eliminated, the State Department concluded that the best way to pacify Germany was to Americanize it; a solution they often extended to other parts of the world. State Department officials tended to believe that the international economy should be restructured into a modern version of a mercantilist empire, although without the political responsibilities that haunted Spain and England. By eliminating trade barriers, all the various national economies could move in what the State Department saw as the natural direction of interdependence. Consciously or not, this form of free trade advocacy would favor the established industrial nations, particularly the United States.

Alternative 4: complete American Occupation. A fourth alternative for postwar Germany—outright occupation by Anglo-American forces before the Soviet army could establish control—was implied in a letter from Roosevelt's erstwhile advisor and personal representative, William C. Bullitt. Following a theme he had developed earlier, Bullitt wrote in August, 1943, of the dilemma posed by trying to keep the Soviet Union in the war since that would permit Stalin to establish Moscow-dominated governments in Germany. Bullitt did not suggest any specific postwar policy for Germany, but his dark warnings of Soviet expansion implied the integration of German industrial and military strength into some sort of anti-Soviet system. Roosevelt had already rejected Bullitt's thesis, but the idea surfaced again once the Anglo-American armies broke through German resistance following the invasion at Normandy in June, 1944. Although Roosevelt remained aware of the possibility that Germany might become communist, either all or in part, he clearly agreed with British Foreign Secretary Anthony Eden's argument that the wise and practical policy would be to develop a friendly and trusting relationship with the Russians, avoiding hostility in every reasonable way. Even with that policy, the president deemed it advisable to have British and American troops either in Germany or ready to go there quickly in the event of a rapid collapse of German resistance. Cooperation with the Soviets was one thing; presenting them with temptations too strong to resist was quite another. The result was an instruction from Roosevelt to make contingency plans which culminated in Operation RANKIN, a plan for an immediate occupation of Germany once Germany surrendered or collapsed. However, such a plan was a far cry from any challenge to Russia's clear-cut political goals, and it stimulated not fear and distrust in Moscow but instead negotiations regarding postwar zones of occupation. RANKIN implied a deep concern over postwar Russian policy, but did not relate to long-term plans for Germany.

Logically, the reconciliation of such alternative policies rested with the chief executive. In fact, Roosevelt refused to commit himself until just before meeting with Churchill in October, 1944. Part of the president's refusal may have stemmed from his personal reluctance to make concrete decisions. Roosevelt's persistent procrastination was partly his politician's unwillingness to say a final no to anyone, but it also indicated his distaste for intensive, analytical thought about any problem. Secretary of War Henry Stimson characterized Roosevelt's mental processes thus:

> His mind does not allow easily a consecutive chain of thought but he is full of stories and incidents and hops about in his discussions from suggestion to suggestion and it is very much like chasing a vagrant beam of sunshine around a vacant room.[1]

A more immediate and practical consideration also influenced the president's refusal to choose between one of the four alternative policies for postwar Germany. His desire to create a lasting cooperative relationship with the Soviet Union, a policy Roosevelt pursued until his death, demanded that major decisions on the future makeup of the world be made only at a postwar peace conference or as a result of face-to-face negotiations with the Russians. As Roosevelt wrote to Churchill in February, 1944:

> I have been worrying a good deal of late on account of the tendency of all of us to prepare for future events in such detail that we may be letting ourselves in for trouble when the time arrives (see Document 7).

The experience of Woodrow Wilson clearly influenced the president's thinking. The famous "secret treaties"—those agreements between the major European allies in World War I in which they divided up the spoils (the Middle East, Africa, and the Pacific islands) even before they were certain of winning the war—had haunted Wilson when he tried to reconstitute a world order along more liberal lines. Though it is likely that the Allies in World War I would have acted similarly in dividing up the colonial world without prior agreements, Roosevelt and most other Wilsonians never forgot the way in which Clemenceau and other negotiators at Paris fenced Wilson in with those treaties. Nor were the Americans and British in a particularly favorable bargaining position in 1944. In spite of the June invasion of Normandy, it was not until 1945 that Allied forces completely broke through German resistance. Until that time the Russians had the best bargaining counters. With the Soviet army on the March by 1944, what had been possible in terms of negotiating with Stalin in 1941 or 1942 was no longer realistic. Roosevelt's refusal in 1944 to make long-term plans for Germany fit neatly into his overall desire to achieve a realistic and hence lasting peace.

Some of the broad goals outlined in the Quebec memorandum initialed by Churchill and Roosevelt were agreed upon by all, even though later disputes arose over methods of implementation. No one argued at the time against disarmament for Germany; denazification and demilitarization of German society have remained part of Anglo-American-Russian policy to this day; and all agreed that some sort of reparations would be required. Only dismemberment and deindustrialization (which were to be made permanent by partitioning) stimulated directly contradictory proposals.

Point of Dissension: Plans for the Dismemberment of Germany

The dismemberment of Germany had been the goal of many French planners since before World War I, and the close proximity of the two world wars left many others convinced that the breakup of Germany was a *sine qua non* for peace. Although most European nations suffered from the same sort of internal disunity that characterized the split between northern (Prussia) and southern (Bavaria) Germany, the very recentness of German unification (the 1860s) made disunity appear that much more reasonable. Even before Roosevelt began to think about it, Soviet Premier Josef Stalin proposed, the separation of the Rhineland and possibly Bavaria from the remainder of Germany. During talks held between Stalin and Anthony Eden in Moscow in December, 1941, the Russians suggested that only such dismemberment could prevent future aggression from Germany. Eden expressed fear that such a punishment could cause an intensification of German nationalism behind a move for reunification, but he did not press the issue.

Such thinking had already made an appearance in the United States. Early in 1941, under Secretary of State Sumner Welles, who often reflected Roosevelt's thinking, suggested to the British ambassador, Lord Halifax, that dismemberment of Germany would be the best way to meet Russia's demands for physical security. Within the State Department, however, few agreed with Welles. Almost from the start, Secretary of State Cordell Hull and the various planning groups within the department opposed any partitioning of Germany. Like Eden, they feared a resurgence of German nationalism in a campaign to restore the nation's integrity, but there is also strong evidence that long-term economic planning played a role in their thinking. Hull and the State Department held firmly to their Wilsonian ideal of a world at peace because of economic equality and prosperity for all, and the division of Germany could interfere with that development. Even when Hull occasionally appeared to support the notion of dismemberment, it was only because he thought it would not prevent economic redevelopment.

Actually, all parties, from the beginning of World War II, had agreed on a partial breakup of Germany. Starting with the initial Eden-Stalin talks in 1941, the Western Allies never seriously opposed Soviet demands that East Prussia be ceded to either Poland or Russia, or both. Moreover, given early Soviet demands for a westward adjustment of the Russo-Polish border, the British and later the Americans soon came to accept some sort of westward shift in the Polish-German border—thus moving the entire Polish state westward, at German expense. Nor was there the slightest doubt that the Sudetenland and Austria would be separated from Germany—in spite of the strong belief in the 1930s that those two areas were economically and culturally part of Germany. Alsace and Lorraine would, of course, be "returned" to France, and some minor territorial adjustment along the Belgian border appeared certain. In a sense, there never existed among the Grand Alliance any rational or ideological commitment to the continued existence of Germany as a nation.

In spite of President Roosevelt's desire to avoid any long-term policy commitments regarding Germany, his offhand remarks indicated the drift of his thinking. The "unconditional surrender" statement made at the Casablanca Conference by Churchill and Roosevelt in January, 1943, called for the capitulation of Germany (as well as Japan and Italy) without any prior conditions or terms, and implied a degree of control over the defeated nation which would allow permanent partitioning. Roosevelt assumed an Allied occupation and told French General Henri Giraud that the desire of Marshal Foch and General Pershing to occupy Germany following World War I had been foolishly denied for political reasons.

Anthony Eden's visit to Washington in March, 1943, prompted the first serious Anglo-American discussions regarding Germany's future (see Document 2). Eden accurately labeled the question of dismemberment as the most important question about post war Germany to resolve. When Roosevelt's close personal advisor, Harry Hopkins, asked Eden and Roosevelt what would happen if a spontaneous anti-Prussian separatist movement did not spring up in Germany, both men agreed that Germany would have to be forcibly divided and that any such dismemberment would include the creation of a separate Prussian state. The relationship of Roosevelt's French and German policies became apparent when the president suggested that a disarmed Germany would obviate the need for the rearming of France. Eden continued to probe and soon found disagreement among American planners. In a conversation with Hull, Eden suggested that dismemberment would be the best policy, but the secretary of state refused to commit himself. Later that same day, when Eden made similar comments to Welles, the American strongly endorsed the idea of a permanent breakup of Germany. Although both Eden and Welles emphasized that they were expressing personal and not official views, the British foreign secretary could see that the United States had not arrived at a fixed policy—in spite of Roosevelt's apparent firmness.

Although the immediacy of military decisions obscured questions of postwar planning during most of 1943, the Churchill-Roosevelt meeting in Washington in May of that year occasioned a plea from Czech President-in-Exile Eduard Benes for the dismemberment of Germany. Shortly thereafter, at a luncheon attended by Vice President Henry Wallace, Secretary of War Henry Stimson, and Under Secretary of State Welles, Prime Minister Churchill spoke of separating Prussia from the remainder of Germany; since forty million Prussians were a manageable unit. He admitted that some people wanted to divide Prussia into even smaller parts but reserved judgment on such proposals.

Roosevelt and The Department of State

Although Hull and the State Department eventually came to be the staunchest opponents of the Morgenthau Plan, Hull's initial attitude regarding postwar Germany clearly indicates that, as in almost everything else, the establishment of worldwide liberal (that is, American-style economic policies dominated his thinking. The only significant discussions concerning Germany which took place at the August, 1943, Quebec conference were between Hull and Eden. Hull specifically asked for Eden's opinion on the question of postwar German unity, and agreed with the foreign minister's comment that dismemberment was not a bad idea but that forced partition was impractical. Eden surmised that only voluntary dismemberment could succeed, and when Hull suggested that giving southern Germany access to the Adriatic Sea through Fiume and Trieste could provide the economic impetus for a separate south German state, Eden and his advisors agreed. Both Hull and Eden worked from the assumption that the Anglo-Americans would not persist in any permanent partitioning scheme and that half-way measures would only stimulate the development of an anti-American, anti-British brand of German nationalism.

Hull's position reflected the conclusions of two lengthy reports sent to the secretary of state on the subjects of "Boundary Problems of Germany" and "Unity or Partition of Germany." The discussion of new boundaries for postwar Germany clearly recommended extensive changes which, in one sense, established a precedent for dismemberment, even though the memorandum claimed to consider boundary questions separately from the issue of partitioning. The second memo, primarily the effort of the department's Advisory Committee on Postwar Policy, examined in detail the two basic alternatives, dismemberment or continued unity. The argument for partition centered on one basic goal—the elimination of Germany's political and economic ability to make war. The defenders of German unity offered three political rationales: that effective controls and safeguards could be constructed which would guarantee a peaceful Germany, that German opposition to dismemberment would require a long-term commitment of occupying troops which Americans opposed, and that German nationalism would bring about a reaction against the peace settlement similar to that which followed the Treaty of Versailles. The report also presented arguments against partition based on the economic role a united Germany could and should play in the reconstruction of the European and world economies, but the specific criticisms of dismemberment centered on the lessons of the post-World War I period—that is, the fear that a punitive peace would only create a Frankenstein monster. Although fears of radicalism or communism in a divided Germany were neither mentioned nor implied in the report, such arguments cropped up soon afterwards. The report offered an alternative which corresponded to the present status of Germany, divided as it is into eastern and western parts, but only in connection with a long series of other possible partitioning schemes.

The growing concern of State Department career diplomats that the Soviet Union would replace Germany as the greatest threat to peace and stability in Europe provided the rationale behind a strong recommendation that United States policy aim at the reintegration of Germany into the European and world community. Written as part of the briefing program for Secretary of State Hull prior to his trip to the Moscow Foreign Minister's Conference in October, 1943, the State Department's Committee on Germany asserted that democratic government in Germany could survive only under three conditions: a decent standard of living, a peace settlement which did not seek revenge, and agreement on policy between the Anglo-Americans and the Russians. The committee believed the Soviet Union had already taken steps to gain control of Germany after the war and that the collapse of democratic postwar government would mean communization. Clearly, the recommendations led American policy in the direction of just what Stalin suspected—a new version of the *cordon sanitaire* against the Soviet Union (see Document 3). Given President Roosevelt's well-known espousal of postwar cooperation between the great powers, it is not surprising that such hard-line views never reached the White House.

Only rarely did Roosevelt openly pursue foreign or domestic policies which lacked a consensus within his circle of close advisors—even if that consensus was coerced and largely rhetorical.[2] Policy on Germany was no exception. State Department postwar planning favored a unified Germany, but not until October, 1943, as part of Secretary Hull's briefing prior to the Moscow Foreign Minister's Conference, did State Department representatives have an opportunity to present their case to the president. With Sumner Welles's resignation as under secretary of state, partition had no influential advocate within the department, and Hull and the others attempted to persuade Roosevelt that partition would not work. The president insisted that

Germany should be divided into three states, although some sort of economic cooperation should be established. Roosevelt claimed that his travels in Germany (made as a schoolboy and as assistant secretary of the navy following World War I) made him an expert and left him convinced that partitioning Germany was the only guaranty of peace. Although the president admitted that perhaps his memories were too old to be valid and that possibly experience might show that partition would not work, he nevertheless clearly wished to try dismemberment before rejecting it (see Document 4).

Although Huil discussed the German question during his talks With Eden and Russian Foreign Minister V.M. Molotov in Moscow, no firm decisions resulted. Neither the British nor the American governments had decided upon a firm German policy at that stage, and the absence of the final authorities—Roosevelt, Churchill, and Stalin—added to the indecision. Hull did present a paper which outlined the American proposal for the treatment of Germany immediately after the declaration of an armistice, but the long-term problems of dismemberment and deindustrialization came up only in the discussions which followed. Eden, following his previously stated ideas, proposed that they encourage voluntary separatism but expressed doubt that forcible partition would work. Hull admitted that dismemberment commanded a majority of supporters within the American government but acknowledged that no decision had been reached. Molotov appeared surprised that the United States did not favor partition more strongly and noted the existence of strong support within the Soviet government for breaking up Germany, but he contented himself with an endorsement of any measures which would guarantee a peaceful Germany. They all agreed to postpone the decision by referring the question to the newly created European Advisory Commission (EAC), but since such major policy could be made only at the highest levels, that referral only swept the problem under the rug.

Reparations, a question which became integrally connected with the future make-up of Germany, came up only at the next to the last session. Hull, who had distributed some position papers on broad economic questions, proposed general guidelines for reparations which specifically aimed at the eventual reconstruction of Germany, thus eliminating reparations as a tool for permanently pacifying that nation.

The overall tone of the Moscow Foreign Ministers Conference and particularly Stalin's promise of eventual aid against Japan elated Roosevelt, fitting neatly into his belief that cooperation with the Russians was both possible and necessary. Yet the details of the meetings apparently made little impact. The cabled reports sent during the conference were no substitute for personal discussions with the president. Yet when Hull returned, Roosevelt was preoccupied with his own planned trip to meet Churchill and Stalin at Teheran. In spite of the fact that Roosevelt had delayed his departure in order to have an opportunity to meet with Hull on the secretary's return from Moscow, their talks consisted of a brief chat in Roosevelt's car on the way back to the capital from Washington National Airport, and a one hour and forty-five minute luncheon meeting the following day. Roosevelt, as Hull somewhat forlornly wrote in his memoirs, "was more interested in discussing the forthcoming conferences at Cairo and at Teheran. He was looking forward to his meeting with Stalin with the enthusiasm of a boy, . . . A few hours later the President was on his way to these historic meetings."[3] Roosevelt did ask Hull for a position paper setting forth the department's views on the postwar treatment of Germany, but Hull had time only to send a copy of the proposal he had submitted at the Moscow Conference, and there is no indication that the president read it or even received it before leaving for the Cairo/Teheran Conferences. If any report did influence Roosevelt's thinking prior to the meetings in Teheran, it was probably a summary of the results of the Foreign Minister's Conference sent to him personally from the American ambassador in Russia, W. Averell Harriman. Roosevelt had always preferred personal reports from his own ambassadors rather than the carefully constructed papers sent to him from the State Department. Harriman's cable reinforced Roosevelt's inclination to support a harsh attitude toward Germany. The ambassador noted that the Russians were even tougher on that question than Britain or America, that they were willing to accept the forcible partition of Germany in order to guarantee their security, and that they believed the Germans should not have a higher standard of living than Russian citizens. Harriman made no personal recommendations, but the overall tone of his message was optimistic about the possibility of cooperation with the Soviet Union. He closed by noting that the Russian representatives had thoroughly convinced him that Soviet flirtation with a Free Germany Committee, which had previously been interpreted by American officials as an attempt to establish a communist government in postwar Germany, was merely propaganda designed to weaken German resistance. Hence Roosevelt left Washington for his meeting with Stalin and Churchill without hearing any real challenge to his own notion of imposing partition, reparations in kind, and a generally tough peace on Germany. Alternative 1, soon to be the Morgenthau Plan, seemed to have the inside track.

Notes

1. Diary of Henry L. Stimson, December 18, 1940, Sterling Memorial Library, Yale University, New Haven, Conn.

2. "Consensus" politics became a perjorative during the administration of Lyndon B. Johnson, even though there is much to recommend it. Under Johnson, who consciously imitated Roosevelt's style, consensus all too often meant the stifling of dissent and unquestioning adherence to the president's position. Under Roosevelt, consensus often meant protracted bickering, bitter arguments over policies, and compromise on all sides. Only occasionally would FDR take charge and directly order an official to toe the mark. This is not to say that the Roosevelt administration was consistently open in its policy-making process, but rather that the president's personal administrative style often resulted in frequent "public" airing of disputes.

3. Cordell Hull, *The Memoirs of Cordell Hull* (London: Hodder & Stoughton, 1948), vol. 2, p. 1313.

2

The Alternatives Take Shape: Germany, from Teheran to Quebec

Roosevelt, the RANKIN Plans, and The Soviet Union

The Teheran Conference in December, 1943, between Roosevelt, Churchill, and Stalin, was the most momentous of the wartime Big Three meetings. Although the Yalta Conference has consistently received more attention, the basic outline of the Yalta agreements took clear shape during the Teheran talks. The status of Western relations with the Soviet Union troubled the deliberations, and most, if not all of the broad policy decisions made Teheran reflected Roosevelt's growing concern for achieving a cooperative relationship between Russia and the Western nations following the war. Evidence, in 1943, of American fears of Soviet postwar policy goals is sparse and ambiguous. Herbert Feis, apparently drawing upon his own experiences in the State Department or upon documents he could not cite, refers to the anxiety of State Department officials about dividing Germany, since that would make it easier for Russia to extend its influence in central Europe. Even Harry Hopkins, who was far more optimistic about the future of Soviet-American relations than most State Department personnel, predicted that, unless some sort of understanding was worked out with Russia and Great Britain, Germany—and possibly Italy and the rest of Europe—would turn either to communism, or anarchy. A greater indicator of such distrust was the policies adopted by the United States for occupied Italy and in the event of a sudden collapse of German resistance—the RANKIN plans.[1]

When, throughout the later summer and fall of 1943, the Russians demanded a meaningful role in the administration of occupied Italy, the United States and Great Britain hemmed, hawed, and finally permitted the Soviet Union to participate in the Allied Control Commission. On paper that seemed to be a substantive concession, but in reality the structure of the Control Commission prevented the Russians from actually playing a meaningful role in the governance of Italy. Whether that explains similar Soviet actions in Eastern Europe, or whether Roosevelt was correct in assuming that Russia would control Eastern Europe regardless of

Anglo-American policy, is not important; what is significant is that American officials consciously excluded the Russians because they feared the expansion of Soviet influence into Italy.

The RANKIN Plans (A, B, and C) were drawn up at the direction of the Anglo-American Combined Chiefs of Staff (CCS)[2] and dealt with the military action required in the event of a partial or total collapse of German resistance. During discussions about that possibility held on board the battleship USS *Iowa* enroute to the Cairo and Teheran meetings, President Roosevelt commented that "there would definitely be a race for Berlin. We may have to put the United States divisions into Berlin as soon as possible." (*Alternative 4:* see Document 5). Harry Hopkins, hardly a knee-jerk anti-Soviet advisor, echoed that sentiment by recommending that the United States be prepared to send in an airborne division on two hours notice. This was not a new notion for Roosevelt. During the Quebec Conference in 1943 Roosevelt had told the Combined Chiefs of Staff that United Nations forces should be prepared to get to Berlin as quickly as the Russians. That clearly implies a political conception behind RANKIN, but it just as clearly shows that the president had no plan to take Berlin *before* the Russians could arrive. The American Joint Chiefs of Staff obviously understood Roosevelt's intentions since they called for collaboration with the Russians in the event of a need to implement RANKIN. Although some American planners may have seen the RANKIN plans as a first step toward a policy of confrontation with the Soviet Union (Alternative 4), Roosevelt did not.

Such conflicting interpretations can be resolved only by inducing certain general policy assumptions made by Franklin Roosevelt. There is ample evidence, here and elsewhere, that he was well aware of the potential threat to American security and interests posed by the Soviet Union in the event of the sort of sudden unconditional surrender of Germany which RANKIN envisaged. He received increasingly strong warnings from his advisors and the State Department along just those lines. Nevertheless, the president also seems to have concluded that a Russo-American confrontation was something to be avoided at any reasonable cost. It made little sense to fight one war in order to plant the seeds of another, and Roosevelt based his policies on that premise. He frequently dodged the tough questions when dealing with the Russians not only because he personally disliked unpleasantness but because he was afraid of getting the wrong answer. Although political leaders are not automatonlike prisoners of their history and institutions, neither can they completely ignore the bureaucracy which supports them. Moreover, Roosevelt was cautious by inclination (as demonstrated by his relatively conservative domestic programs, even at the height of the Great Depression), and consistently hedged his bets. He adopted a broad policy of cooperation with the Soviet Union, yet he regularly tried to cover himself in case such cooperation failed. A prime example is his refusal to implement a policy of economic coercion against the Russians, using Lend-Lease[3] and the question of postwar reconstruction loans as bait. He may have learned something from the disastrous effects of such economic pressure on Japan prior to the Pearl

Harbor attack. It is certain that he drew back from such policies during World War II, in spite of repeated and emphatic recommendations from advisors. So it is with RANKIN and Roosevelt's decisions regarding control of occupied Italy. He had no desire to "take" Berlin in order to keep the Soviet forces out; he merely wanted to hedge his bets and insure that American forces would be in a position to guarantee that the Russians would not move into a vacuum. In Italy he apparently assumed that Russian demands for an administrative role were largely rhetorical and that the Soviet leaders hardly expected the United States to ask them in. Since he was willing to grant the Russians dominance in Eastern Europe, Roosevelt believed he could be tougher in Italy without destroying the cooperative relationship he hoped to establish.

Conference at Teheran

Nothing happened at the Teheran Conference to alter substantially the vague but general Allied agreement to dismember Germany. It is difficult, however, to determine why the question of Germany's future took so little of their time, even though the Big Three leaders agreed that it was the most important postwar problem. Stalin did take the initiative early in the talks, demanding strict, long-term measures to prevent the redevelopment of militarism and criticizing as ineffective Churchill's suggestion of constant supervision over German industry. Although the Russian premier did not call for the elimination of German industry, he moved in that direction when he pointed out that peacetime production could all too easily be converted into arms production. Joining security with punishment, Stalin remarked that he strongly disagreed with Churchill's distinction between German leaders and the German people. Stalin argued that German prisoners he himself had interrogated invariably defended their abuses of civilians as obedience to orders. His points were clear: obedience was no excuse for German atrocities, and such a cowardly people would always be easy prey to every militaristic demagogue who came along.

Stalin's distrust of the German people antedated World War II, for he condemned the failure of German workers to break out of their obedient mentality and support revolution, citing an incident in 1907 when German workers had not climbed aboard a train going to a rally because no conductor at the railroad station would punch their tickets. Stalin insisted that Germany would, unless rigidly controlled, make a complete recovery in fifteen or twenty years, and he labeled President Roosevelt's proposal for intervention by the major powers (Roosevelt called them the Four Policemen) an inadequate substitute for an occupation of Germany. Roosevelt quickly agreed. The president and Stalin likewise concluded that factories could all too easily be converted to military production; the Russian again pointed out that such shifts could readily be concealed from outsiders. Stalin repeated those sentiments at a formal dinner the following day and coupled them with a remark to Churchill that between 50,000 and 100,000 Germans ought to be executed. Although Roosevelt quickly tried to turn the comment into a joke by suggesting that only 49,000 members of the German Commanding Staff be liquidated, Stalin's prior brutal treatment of his opponents within the Soviet Union argues for his seriousness.

A few days later, Roosevelt brought up his proposal for the dismemberment of Germany into five small states plus two regions under international or United Nations control: the Ruhr/Saar and the Kiel Canal/Hamburg areas.[4] Churchill demurred and returned to one of the old stand-by proposals for the reconstruction of Central and Eastern Europe: confederation. The prime minister agreed that Prussia should be a separate state but suggested that southern Germans be united in a general Danubian Confederation. The Russians had long realized that such confederation proposals were directed towards limiting Soviet influence in Eastern Europe as much as towards establishing political and economic stability, Stalin immediately rejected Churchill's proposal as both artificial and dangerous, claiming the Germans might well gain control of such a confederation. Roosevelt agreed with Stalin's argument that there was little to choose between Prussians and other Germans and mused that Germany had posed less of a threat to civilization when it consisted of 107 provinces. Since Stalin had already acknowledged that he preferred a Germany made up of many little states, Churchill—seeing himself outnumbered—shifted the discussion to other matters. At that point Roosevelt noted that they still had not referred the dismemberment question to any study group, and all agreed that the European Advisory Commission should examine the problem (see Document 6).

So the German question lay unresolved at the close of the Teheran Conference. But why? Certainly part of the reason was that OVERLORD, the projected Anglo-American invasion of German-held France, dominated the political and military discussions at the meeting. That the invasion of the Normandy peninsula, so long delayed, was clearly Stalin's greatest concern, and Soviet negotiators exerted great efforts to pin the Americans down to a specific date and commander and force the reluctant British formally to endorse the invasion. Nevertheless, that does not explain the vagueness and indecisiveness of the talks on Germany. The real reason was the distrust and political tension which existed among the governments of the three nations. Anglo-American conflict had arisen over questions of British colonialism and American economic expansion, and there was a vague but persistent American fear that Churchill hoped permanently to entangle America in European power politics, thus permitting Britain to expand her own influence. As Lord Moran, Churchill's personal physician and confidant, put it:

> To the Americans the P.M. [Prime Minister] is the villain of the piece; they are far more sceptical of him than they are of Stalin. Anyway, whoever is to blame, it is clear that we are going to Teheran without a common plan.[5]

Given Roosevelt's earnest desire to create an atmosphere of cooperation and trust which would live on after the war, it is little wonder that he consistently made concessions to Stalin in order to create and preserve that sense of harmony; just as Wilson had made concessions to French Premier Clemenceau following World War I. Conflicts between the Americans and British were more on the order of family quarrels; quarrels which could, if necessary, be resolved almost preremptorily by the Americans—the breadwinner. Already faced with Stalin-Roosevelt unity in principle on the question of a massive invasion of occupied France instead of Churchill's Mediterranean strategy, the British had to play a third-man-out role for the remainder of the conference. The issue of Germany was no exception. The Russians had indicated a preference for dismemberment almost from the outset of the war, and that fit neatly with Roosevelt's personal inclinations as well as with his policy of cooperation. Nonetheless, Roosevelt did not want to see British opposition to extensive partitioning of Germany become a truly divisive issue among the Big Three. His recommendation that the EAC consider the problem was obviously designed to end the discussion and avoid forcing the issue with Churchill.

Stalin's motives are, as ever, more difficult to determine. His heated references to the unworthy character of the German worker indicates that his overiding concern for the physical security of Russia against German militarism was not feigned. Nor did he ever demand or even suggest anything resembling permanent Russian control of any portion of Germany, except for the accepted share of East Prussia. Stalin's uncertainty was more likely a function of his priorities. The future of Poland and Eastern Europe was far more crucial, and the Soviet position on Germany depended upon those issues. Anglo-American disagreement provided Stalin with an opportunity to extend Soviet influence if that was his policy, but it is more likely that such disagreement only left him confused and reluctant to make specific commitments.

Still, a few things about Germany appeared settled. Even Churchill had agreed that Prussia should be separated from the rest of Germany, and he and Stalin reaffirmed decisions reached at the Moscow Foreign Ministers' Conference to put German war criminals on trial at the locations where the crimes had been committed. Most important, the three agreed not to disagree, at least for the time being. Intriguingly, the basic issue which would underlie the Morgenthau Plan—deindustrialization—had been raised by Stalin and seconded by Roosevelt, though Churchill was less enthusiastic; all nine months before the actual birth of the Morgenthau Plan itself.

The Unconditional Surrender Policy

But merely raising issues was about as far as Franklin Roosevelt wished to go on the question of policy for postwar Germany. As he put it in a letter to Churchill written two months after the Teheran Conference:

> I have been worrying a good deal of late on account of the tendency of all of us to prepare for future events in such detail that we may be letting ourselves in for trouble when the time arrives (see Document 7).

Even so, certain basic ideas regarding Germany remained constant in Roosevelt's thinking. During the Teheran talks, Stalin had suggested that the

Allied policy of Unconditional Surrender might prolong German resistance. Although he did not pursue the subject, Churchill and the British picked up that theme a few weeks after Roosevelt had returned to the United States. The president's reaction was unusually unequivocal. He strongly condemned "Nazism and Prussian militarism and the fantastic and disastrous notion that they constitute the 'Master Race.' "[6]

The Unconditional Surrender policy, jointly agreed upon by Churchill and Roosevelt during the Casablanca Conference in January, 1943, served two goals: to reassure the Russians of Anglo-American intentions in the absence of a second front in Western Europe, and to guarantee a complete and convincing defeat of the German military establishment.

The first of these goals demonstrated the general state of tension which existed between the Russians and the Allies. From the outset of the war, Soviet leaders had demanded the opening of a major second front in western Europe in order to take pressure off the Russian army. Soviet Foreign Minister Molotov visited London and Washington in May, 1942, with the purpose of obtaining a firm commitment to just such a front. In spite of Churchill's strong warnings, Roosevelt grandly promised an Anglo-American invasion of Western Europe, possibly as early as the fall of 1941—a military impossibility. Roosevelt's purpose in making such a commitment was political, for it was coupled with a sweeping verbal picture of a postwar world protected and nurtured by the "Big Four" (Britain, China, Russia, and the United States), acting in harmony and partnership. This vision, designed to hold the wartime alliance together by convincing the Russians that the Western powers could be trusted, ultimately degenerated into sleight of hand and procrastination by war's end, but Unconditional Surrender lived on.

The second purpose behind the Unconditional Surrender policy sprang from the president's interpretation of how World War II began. Put in the simplest terms, which was invariably how Roosevelt put it, the war came about because of Prussian militarism and the overall German acceptance of Hitler's expansionist program. Hemmed in by his reading of history, Roosevelt believed that only a total defeat and the resultant discrediting of the German military establishment could prevent a rebirth of the old post-World War I myth that the German civilians (mainly the socialists) had stabbed the army in the back in 1919, thus preventing a victory. Franklin Roosevelt's personal distaste and disgust for the German military in particular and the German "race" in general permeates his wartime letters and memoranda. When the fate of postwar Germany came up at the Teheran meeting, the president's initial reaciton was to suggest that the concept and even the word "reich" should be stricken from the German language. Although this can be interpreted as opposition to German unity, it also exhibited a strongly emotional anti-German attitude. Stalin's comment that he saw little to choose between Prussians and other Germans received a quick second from Roosevelt, who added that such differences had disappeared since the First World War. The president's later insistence that plans for postwar Germany include the specific outlawing of the goose-step is an almost ludicrous extension of his loss of faith in the German people as a whole. Although it is possible that insistence upon Unconditional Surrender, long after it had outlived its usefulness as a form of political glue for the wartime alliance, came from Roosevelt's desire to avoid hard decisions on Germany until American policy was decided upon, the most consistent motive behind the policy was fear of German military expansion. To the president and many American leaders, the destruction of the prestige of the German military was not merely an alternative—it was a firm decision.

As tenuous and vague as the Cairo and Teheran agreements on Germany were, Roosevelt acted as if everything had been settled. Dismemberment had received Big Three support, as had the concept of an occupation of Germany; war criminals would be punished; and aboard the USS *Iowa* enroute to the talks, the president had made clear to the military his desire that the zones of occupation roughly coincide with natural political and geographic sub-divisions of Germany, which could then become three to five permanently separated German states. Specific occupation policies could be developed at a later date when military questions were less pressing and in the meantime the European Advisory Commission could prepare reports and recommendations on such matters.

It appeared simple and logical but did not work that way. Three problems intervened. First, the American members of the EAC did not know of the president's insistence on the United States occupying the northwestern zone in Germany. Second, military planning for the invasion of Normandy (OVERLORD) had assigned the American forces to the southern sector from where they were ultimately supposed to move across France into southern, not northwestern, Germany. Moreover, the logistical build-up for the invasion (code named BOLERO) had already proceeded on the latter assumption. Third, the planning impulse within the bureaucracy was too ingrained and strong to wait for Franklin Roosevelt or events to resolve the unanswered questions.

Not only did Roosevelt insist that the EAC perform strictly in an advisory capacity, but he also assumed that his policy decisions on surrender terms and zones of occupation had reached the American representative on the commission, his ambassador in Great Britain, John Winant. The president had instructed Harry Hopkins to provide the guidance Winant needed, but Hopkin's ill health following the Teheran Conference prevented his carrying out those instructions. Roosevelt's objections to an American zone of occupation in southern Germany came in response to a British proposal, which was made in the summer of 1943. He had agreed with the notion of three separate zones of occupation but adamantly demanded the north-western zone for the United States (see Documents 5 and 8). His reasoning was, as always, impressionistic though not without logic.

Roosevelt had repeatedly indicated both a strong distrust of British political motives and a fear that the southern zone would make France the responsibility of the United States. Since he and his then close advisor, Admiral William Leahy, believed that France would be torn by civil war and would require both policing and extensive economic aid, the president insisted that the British take the southern zone, which was contiguous to France. Throughout 1944, until they settled the dispute during the second Quebec Conference in September of that year, Churchill and Roosevelt exchanged frequent and heated messages on the question of assigning occupation zones. The crux of the president's position was that the United States could not, should not, and would not become permanently involved in spheres of influence in France or anywhere else in Europe. Roosevelt's almot mechanical application of his Four Policemen concept meant that European questions were the responsibility of Great Britain and the Soviet Union, for American forces would be withdrawn from Europe within one to two years after the war's end (see Document 7).

The most complete and troublesome exposition of Roosevelt's views on zones came in conjunction with the conference he held with his Joint Chiefs of Staff aboard the USS *Iowa*, just prior to the Cairo meeting with Churchill in November, 1943. At the end of the discussion, the president crudely sketched the zonal boundaries he wanted on a *National Geographic* map of Europe. The sketch gave the northwestern zone to the United States and included Berlin, although all of the president's earlier remarks as well as a later version of the map submitted to Roosevelt indicate that he favored a joint occupation of the German capital. Although the map and the conference notes did not reach the EAC, the British Chiefs of Staff received notice of the proposal and immediately set to work developing arguments in favor of a British zone in the northwest. On January 14, 1944, at the first official meeting of the EAC, those arguments surfaced.

The Alternative of Unified Occupation—Rejected

The American representatives on the EAC could not respond to the British initiative and quickly found themselves even more embarrassed when the Russians made a similar proposal, which called for three zones plus a tripartite occupation of Berlin. In essence, that eliminated one variation of the alternatives available to the United States (*Alternative 3:* see Document 8). Even though Roosevelt had strongly and consistently supported dismemberment of Germany, some planners within the State Department as well as General Dwight D. Eisenhower, Supreme Allied Commander in Europe, had considered the option of a tripartite occupation of all of Germany, thus eliminating separate zones. Regardless of the advantages of such a plan, Anglo-Russian agreement on the western boundary of the Soviet zone meant that Roosevelt, who favored zones as a first step toward partitioning, would have to challenge directly Stalin and Churchill; an unlikely possibility given the president's goal of postwar cooperation with the Russians. Thus, quietly and without notice, consideration of the only alternative to zones—zones whose boundaries eventually became the lines of divided Germany—became impossible. Roosevelt's instructions to the State Department, repeated to Winant in London for his guidance, accepted by implication the Soviet zone's western boundary and argued only about the Anglo-American occupation areas (see Document 8). Churchill and Roosevelt continued to argue the question until the Quebec Conference that fall, but its resolution proved less significant than the final acceptance of the concept of zones of occupation.

Franklin Roosevelt's administrative style made for uncertainty and competition within the American government, and the jealousy which characterized relations between the War and State departments finds no better illustration than in planning for Germany. Lack of coordination between the two bureaucracies resulted in a clash when the army planners forwarded a zonal boundary proposal based upon Roosevelt's original sketch. Initially reluctant to let the EAC discuss what they considered military matters, War Department officials finally decided to make a contribution lest the EAC work only from State Department directives. Since the original proposal called for a Soviet boundary far to the east of the one already accepted, the War Department suggestion caused some consternation and anger among the Americans on the EAC. It took a trip to Washington by Winant's counselor in the London embassy, George F. Kennan, to work that out. Although Roosevelt reacted to the confusion with amusement, the incident placed a noticeable strain on relations between the two departments. That was only a prelude to a more acrimonious dispute; this time over the broad question of postwar policy during the occupation of Germany and involving the Treasury Department as well.

War Department planning for the occupation of postwar Germany began largely as a result of unhappy memories among senior officers in the army over the disorganized military response to the occupation of the Philippine Islands in 1902, Veracruz, Mexico, in 1914, and Germany in 1917. By 1943 Secretary of War Henry Stimson and Army Chief of Staff George Marshall had established a military government school and a Civil Affairs Division within the War Department. The military administration of occupied Italy provided a precedent and early in 1944 specific plans began to emanate from within the military bureaucracy. In spite of the army's insistence that it could deal only with questions of short-term military occupation policy, common sense indicated that even contigency plans should reflect long-term thinking. Since it appeared that reparations, the need to support both the German population and the occupying forces, and the war effort against Japan necessitated continued German production, War Department planners assumed the continued operation of the German industrial plant.

Military planning for the occupation of Germany finally produced a joint Anglo-American policy directive. Supplemented by other plans but never replaced, the instruction (titled "Combined Directive for Military Government in Germany Prior to Defeat or Surrender" and abbreviated as CCS 551) was issued by the Combined Chiefs of Staff as official guidance for the Supreme Commander of the Allied Expeditionary Forces in Europe (SCAEF), General Eisenhower (*Alternative 2:* see Document 9). As with all army/War Department plans, it called for complete freedom of action for the military governors. Ostensibly not intended to deal with long-term political questions, CCS 551 offered no barriers to increasingly strong State Department support for the reintegration of Germany into the European and world economy.

In spite of the seemingly innocuous and even sympathetic War Department position, State Department planners looked askance at CCS 551 and any other military plans for postwar Germany. The reason was simple—bureaucratic jealousy. In late November, 1941, Secretary of State Hull had told Stimson that affairs were in the hands of the military for the duration—but that statement had an implied corollary: once the war ended, the Department of State would deal with foreign relations. In the eyes of State Department officials, planning for postwar Germany was their bailiwick, and trespassing would not be tolerated. Highly sensitive to President Roosevelt's frequent bypassing of Secretary Hull and of established bureaucratic channels within the foreign policy-making establishment, State Department personnel struggled with increasing vigor to assert their views. They established the Working Security Committee as a means of securing War Department approval for State Department plans, even though the stated goal of the committee was coordination between the two departments. When that failed because of the refusal of the Joint Chiefs of Staff to give up their authority over occupation policies, the State Department moved to revise its standing position on postwar Germany—the position paper given earlier to the British and the Russians during the 1943 Moscow Conference. Department instructions to Winant in London made clear that German industry should contribute to the rehabilitation of the European economy in the postwar period; a viewpoint which Winant strongly endorsed. In fact, Winant went a step further and recommended that representatives of all the European nations study the question of economic policy toward Germany, since their economies were intertwined. Finally, during the summer of 1944, Hull forwarded to the Joint Chiefs of Staff, Secretary of War Stimson, and Roosevelt two long memoranda outlining the department's recommendations for postwar economic and political policy toward Germany.

The State Department program melded traditional American liberal capitalism—what historian Bruce Kuklick has called multilateralism—with the economic and social planning approach which characterized a major aspect of the New Deal (*Alternative 3:* see Documents 10 and 11). Although the plan endorsed security measures required to prevent a rebirth of German militarism, it rejected the argument that long-term restrictions on German industrial capability could achieve that goal. Yet, in what is a seeming contradiction, the State Department proposed a system whereby the German economy would be controlled as required by world security considerations. The key to reconciling these contradictory positions is the department's ultimate policy—the re-creation of the world in the American image. Convinced that the firm application of American political, economic, and social principles would reform the German tendency toward militarism and economic selfishness, State Department planners assumed that controls over the German economy could eventually be lifted once the Germans had adopted the American economic system. In the meantime, the German people would be reeducated and their economy redirected so that, in the words of the memo; "German economic self-sufficiency for war must be replaced by an economy which can be integrated into an inter-dependent world economy" (see Document 10). In other words, American policy would dictate what direction the postwar German economy would take.

This was not the plan of evil men who aimed at the exploitation of the world for America's benefit. Rather, it was the logical conclusion of people who believed firmly that only the creation of a world-wide system which combined republican governments with American style free enterprise economics could bring about permanent peace and prosperity. These planners had no great affection for the Germans, as Hull's later actions indicate, but they refused to let wartime emotions govern their postwar planning. As the war progressed, more people argued that a harsh peace would open Germany to bolshevism, but in mid-1944 the State Department planners dreamed of far more than just the negative goals of containment. They were determined to seize the opportunity which had eluded their intellectual father, Woodrow Wilson. This time a spirit of revenge and demands for a Carthaginian peace would not frustrate the creation of a *novus ordo seclorum*—a new world order.

Ironically, the strongest challenge to the State Department program came not from the military, which cared primarily about immediate control and order rather than long-term policy, but from another group of bureaucrats who also considered the peace settlement following World War I a failure and who vowed to do better.

Treasury Department representatives at the EAC in London had reported, as early as July 15, 1944, that American and British diplomats apparently assumed that German industry should be rehabilitated and restored as a major element in the European economy. On August 6, 1944, Secretary of the Treasury Henry Morgenthau read the State Department plan and labeled it "a nice WPA job."[7] Within a few weeks he advanced the alternative of the planned and calculated destruction of German industry—the Morgenthau Plan for Germany *(Alternative 1)*.

Notes

1. See p. 000 for an explanation of the RANKIN plans.

2. The Combined Chiefs of Staff was the joint Anglo-American organization representing the British and American Military Chiefs of Staff.

3. Lend-Lease was the major World War II foreign and military aid program established in 1941 by the United States to support its allies, particularly Britian and Russia.

4. The five states were: (1) a small Prussia, (2) Hanover and the northwest, (3) Saxony/Leipzig, (4) Hesse-Darmstadt, Hesse-Kassel, and south of the Rhine River, and (5) Bavaria, Baden, and Württemberg.

5. Lord Moran (Sir Charles Wilson), *Churchill: Taken from the Diaries of Lord Moran; The Struggle for Survival, 1940-1965* (Boston: Houghton Mifflin Co., 1966), p. 142.

6. Roosevelt to Churchill, January 6, 1944, Map Room Collection, #436, Franklin D. Roosevelt Papers, Franklin D. Roosevelt Library, Hyde Park, New York.

7. Statement by Morgenthau to the Subcommittee to Investigate the Administration of the Internal Security Act and Other Internal Security Laws of the Committee on Judiciary, U.S., Congress, Senate, 90th Cong., 1st sess., August 17, 1944, in *Morgenthau Diary (Germany),* 2 vols. (Washington, D.C.: U.S. Government Printing Office, 1967), vol. 1, p. 414.

3

The Morgenthau Plan: The Internationalization of the Agrarian Myth

Morgenthau and those who supported his plan for the pastoralization of Germany could not have predicted the political and economic ramifications of what they proposed. Full implementation would have meant the neutralization of Germany, something which would have integrally changed the structure of the Cold War equation. Whether European economic prosperity depended upon German industrial recovery is both doubtful and moot; that equation became a self-fulfilling prophecy since American policy-makers ultimately acted as if that was the case.

The People Behind The Plan

In reality, Henry Morgenthau, Jr. acted primarily out of a very deep and honest hatred for Germany and a sense of moral outrage. Convinced that Naziism represented the logical conclusion of German nationalism, racism, and anti-Semitism, the Treasury Secretary fought to eliminate permanently the German state and German war-making potential. Morgenthau's intense feelings are only partially explained by his Jewishness. In fact, given Hitler's atrocities it seems more significant to ask why virtually all Americans and their government officials did not feel the same way. Morgenthau had displayed strong interest in Jewish refugee problems and had, with assistance from his staff, forced the American government to confront its own hypocritical policy of extending only verbal assistance to such refugees. His commitment to that issue and to his plan for Germany both exhibit one of his primary personal characteristics? he was a very sensitive and humane man. His career as a close friend and aide to Franklin Roosevelt is replete with examples of that humaneness. Although the Morgenthau Plan for Germany later received widespread condemnation as a design to starve the German people, that was not his intention. A gentlemen farmer who loved the land (his early work with Roosevelt had been in agriculture), Morgenthau assumed that reestablishing contact with the land would turn the Germans into good, honest, democratic yeomen farmers, the Jeffersonian ideal. He, along with Roosevelt, rejected as artificial the State Department's distinction between

Germans and Nazis. Always a believer in the agrarian myth, he sought to eliminate the temptations of an industrial society so that the German people could reform themselves. Since hard-working farmers would never starve, Morgenthau rejected the accusations that the plan called for the destruction of the German people. At one conference Morgenthau compared his concept with the general social structure in Denmark; "where the people, through small-scale farming, were in intimate association with the land and were peace-loving and without aggressive designs upon others."[1] Morgenthau went on to claim that he envisaged a program somewhat similar to those of the Rural Resettlement and Farm Security Administrations during the New Deal. The Morgenthau Plan for Germany assumed that the Germans deserved harsh punishment, but its ultimate thrust was as an extension of the New Deal reform impulse.

Morgenthau's assistants, many of whom played a key role in the development of the plan for Germany, reflected his views for a variety of reasons. As Treasury Secretary for ten years, Morgenthau had naturally surrounded himself with people who tended to think as he did. Moreover, the secretary engendered intense loyalty among his subordinates and repaid the debt in kind. Some were Jewish and possibly inclined to a deep personal involvement regarding Germany. Some, including the controversial Harry Dexter White, had become concerned over the chances of an "easy" peace even before Morgenthau.

White, the most influential of Morgenthau's advisors, later became the target of accusations made by various congressional investigating committees. Flimsy and uncorroborated statements made by a few witnesses before those groups, inspired speculations that White had formulated the Morgenthau Plan on orders from Moscow. That is simply not true. White played a most important role, but Morgenthau provided the basic inspiration. Moreover, White's key role in the negotiation of the Bretton Woods agreements regarding postwar international monetary policies found him supporting positions which were directly opposed to Soviet policy.

In the case of the Morgenthau Plan, White stands accused by one group of writing a plan designed to fit in with Soviet foreign policy, and by another of consistently following, along with Morgenthau, goals which were clearly anti-Russian. The facts do not bear out either interpretation. White and Morgenthau supported Roosevelt's program of cooperation with the Soviet Union and at times went even further than the president in that direction. Yet both men firmly believed in America's liberal capitalism and, particularly in the area of monetary policy, acted to reinforce and expand that system. As will be discussed later, Russian policy regarding postwar Germany took many twists and turns but only briefly did it resemble the Morgenthau Plan. If White had instructions to reflect Soviet policy, then he did a poor job of it.

Morgenthau's first contact with the State Department proposal for postwar Germany came when White handed him a copy while they were aboard an airplane enroute to London. Morgenthau reacted angrily, and what began as an "inspection" trip with the ostensible purpose of discussing currency questions in liberated France, quickly developed into a series of conferences to discuss postwar planning for Germany. As soon as he arrived in England, Morgenthau tried to pin down General Eisenhower. In language reminiscent of the War Department position papers, the Supreme Allied Commander indicated a strong belief in treating the Germans sternly, particularly in the matter of discrediting their military establishment, but avoided any meaningful discussion of long-term political questions.

The British Position

The American representative on the European Advisory Commission, Ambassador Winant, argued that opinion in Britain followed three lines of thought, with each group's attitude toward the Soviet Union the determining factor in its recommendations regarding Germany. Foreign Secretary Eden led those who believed that only cooperation with the Russians could bring about a peaceful postwar situation, and since the Russians demanded a harsh policy toward Germany, the British did the same. Churchill and his supporters, though more dubious about coexistence with the Soviet Union, would not oppose Roosevelt. A third faction staunchly held that communism posed a greater threat than a militaristic Germany and proposed building a series of European alliances based upon a strong Germany and a strong France. More significantly, Winant and other State Department officials then in England and Robert Sherwood, one of Roosevelt's speechwriters, argued that Roosevelt had not made any final decisions.

The British reaction to Morgenthau's queries regarding postwar planning for Germany left the Treasury Secretary with   false impression of strong support. Eden agreed with Winant's evaluation of Britain's debates over postwar German policy but claimed that Churchill had reluctantly agreed to follow the policy decisions made at Teheran. Surprised at the Americans' seeming ignorance of the general agreement on Germany reached at that conference Eden claimed that the British planned a stern policy toward Germany and offered to let Morgenthau read the British minutes taken at Teheran. Winant, Morgenthau, and Eden claimed that agreement on policy for Germany among the Big Three was more important than their own personal desires. The impression left by Eden's strong statements received reinforcement when Brendan Bracken, British minister of information and one of Churchill's closest friends, asserted that a soft peace might push the Russians in the direction of some sort of deal with the Germans. Bracken supported drastic dismemberment of Germany, including the establishment of a Rhineland republic and the transfer of territory to France.

first emphatic indication of British concern over reparations came when Sir William Strang, the British delegate on the EAC, explained that the commission had looked at the partitioning question from an economic point of view. Strang pointed out that a divided Germany could not provide reparations and that the administrative problems caused by dealing with a multitude of German governments meant that Germany should remain united in the early occupation stages. Eden and Morgenthau responded that the policy. discussions at Teheran, which the foreign minister had just shown to Morgenthau, clearly indicated that the EAC should draw up its economic and political plans on the assumption that Germany would be partitioned (see Document 12). According to Morgenthau's recollections, one State Department representative, Philip Mosely, argued vehemently that a harsh peace and radical dismemberment of Germany would force the Germans to accept the Soviet embrace. Although White's notes of that conversation do not verify this argument, later events demonstrated that the specter of the bolshevization of Germany clearly affected British and American thinking.

The only point of complete agreement among Morgenthau, the State Department members of the EAC, and the British was that clarification from Roosevelt had to come, and quickly, because Allied armies had made remarkable progress since the Normandy landings. Anglo-American forces had broken the German lines in early August and by the time Morgenthau returned to Washington on August 17, Allied forces were less than forty miles from Paris. With the possibility looming of a RANKIN situation (the collapse of Germany military resistance), Morgenthau feared that military planning for the occupation would no longer await political guidance.

Although Morgenthau had interpreted Eisenhower's condemnation of the enemy as support for deindustrialization, the general's true beliefs are better illustrated by a memo he sent to his advance command post three weeks after meeting with Morgenthau. Concerned primarily with law and order, the message speculated that the German economy could well collapse during the initial occupation period and went on to suggest that therefore the military should not assume the task of supporting and controlling Germany. In other words, the military wanted political decisions which could either prevent such a collapse of order or absolve it from any responsibility. Though Eisenhower made no such recommendation, the inference was that law and order, the primary goal of the military, could not survive an economic collapse.

Aware that such pressures could decide the issue without further debate, Morgenthau wasted no time. After a quick and ultimately unsuccessful attempt to recruit the support of Secretary of State Hull, Morgenthau went directly to the top. During a half-hour meeting with Roosevelt, he summarized his discussions with Churchill, Eden, Eisenhower, and the members of the EAC. Morgenthau began by relating Churchill's unsettling statement that England was "broken" (see Document 13). This proved a shrewd tactic, since the president expressed real surprise and concern and eventually began to see an industrialized Germany as a continued threat to British economic stability. When Morgenthau explained that the State Department and the British members of the EAC had not developed plans for a harsh occupation policy, the president's response was crude but revealing:

We have got to be tough with Germany and I mean the German people, not just the Nazis. You either have to castrate the German people or you have got to treat them in such a manner so they can't just go on reproducing people who want to continue the way they have in the past.

When Morgenthau pointed out that the British wanted to rebuild Germany so that they could collect reparations, Roosevelt contemptuously dismissed the idea. Morgenthau complained that the military had planned for Germany as if it were a relief and rehabilitation project by the WPA, in spite of Eisenhower's apparent toughness, and when the secretary remarked that the army had tacitly agreed on an American zone in southern Germany, the president simply commented that he did not care so long as France was not left "in his lap" (*Alternative 1:* see Document 13).

Roosevelt Inclines Toward the Plan

Although Roosevelt made no commitment to action during the conversation with Morgenthau, the implications were clear: the German people deserved punishment, the rebuilding of Germany's industrial strength should not occur, the small but thorny question of the assignment of specific zones of occupation no longer stood in the way of Anglo-American cooperation, the United States had no interest in reparations, and the precarious state of the British economy concerned the president deeply.

Morgenthau's initial action after the talk with Roosevelt was to appoint a departmental committee charged with putting together an extensive presentation of the treasury's proposal for postwar Germany. Although a few Treasury Department officials, notably Robert E. McConnell, proposed transferring most major German industries to American ownership rather than razing them, Morgenthau took personal command of the planning and directed the Committee to develop plans for dismemberment and deindustrialization.

Major policy decisions during the Roosevelt administrations came only after the inevitable bureaucratic war, and while the Treasury Department labored over what would be known as the Morgenthau Plan for Germany the first skirmishes in that battle occurred. Morgenthau was the hands-down winner. He passed on to the president a "Handbook of Military Government for Germany" written by Allied military planners in London, along with a memo which highlighted the handbook's emphasis upon "the gradual rehabilitation of peacetime industry," the conversion of industry from wartime to peacetime production, a centralized German administration, and the development of plans to provide the German people with a minimum food intake of two thousand calories per day (*Alternative 2:* see Document 14). Obviously annoyed, the president issued instructions to Stimson that the handbook be revised. Complaining that the plan seemed to call for the restoration of Germany as if it were Belgium instead of thinking in terms of soup kitchens, the president stated that he saw no reason for beginning any major relief program for the Germans along the lines of the WPA, CCC, or PWA.[2]

Forced by military events and bureaucratic pressures to choose between two alternative policies for Germany, Roosevelt tended toward the position he had vaguely supported from the outset of the war—a harsh, punitive, and forcible peace imposed upon Germany. This was to be another *diktat*[3] like the Versailles Treaty, only this time it would work by permanently eliminating Germany's ability to wage war. If Roosevelt considered the contradiction between the commitment required in order to impose such a peace and his repeated refusals to entangle the United States in Europe's postwar political problems, he never put his thoughts on paper. Possibly he reconciled the two by assuming that the pastoralization of Germany would obviate the need for any sort of long-term political role for the United States in Germany—though that did not answer the question of how Germany was to be prevented from rebuilding its industrial machine and reuniting. Like Woodrow Wilson, Roosevelt tended to hide behind internationalism in order to avoid any confrontation with the dilemma of creating an American world without deep political involvement. Wilson escaped reality by believing that the League of Nations would solve such problems; Roosevelt, as evidenced by a conversation with Morgenthau, envisaged himself in the role of elder world statesman working with the United Nations Organization.[4]

The Morgenthau Plan for Germany, written by the Treasury Department staff and finally titled "Program to Prevent Germany from Starting a World War III," appeared in essentially final form by September 4, 1944 (*Alternative 1:* see Documents 15 and 16). Divided into two broad sections, the plan outlined long-term policies regarding dismemberment, deindustrialization, denazification, and demilitarization, and followed with a section on the problem of punishing war criminals. The demilitarization clause called for not only the complete disarming of all Germans but the elimination and/or destruction of those industries essential to the development of military power. The keys to achieving that goal were the dismantling and destruction of all industry and mines in the Ruhr, the establishment of international administration over the Ruhr, and a prohibition against long-term or recurrent reparations—this last provision designed to head off any arguments that long-term reparations required the preservation of German industry. Although no specific reforms were mentioned in the outline, it laid the groundwork for social change by forbidding any educational or news dissemination activities until the appropriate teachers, textbooks, and directions were available. Fearful of inadvertent action by the military which would resuscitate the German economy in the name of law, order, and efficiency, the Morgenthau Plan flatly forbade the military to take any policy-making role in German economic affairs except insofar as was necessary for military operations, i.e., the war against Japan. Reflecting Roosevelt's (and the American public's) preference for avoiding long-term political/military commitments in Europe, the proposal called for the policing of Germany by her neighbors and for the relatively speedy withdrawal of American troops. Oddly out of place amidst such broad proposals were specific prohibitions against uniforms, military bands, marching, and all aircraft—each a point specifically requested by the president and carefully inserted on Morgenthau's instructions.

The war crimes section was unyieldingly harsh, though more logical and less hypocritical than the war crimes trials which later took place. "Arch-criminals" whose names appeared on a master list would be summarily executed upon identification, and the mandatory death penalty would apply for any person who caused the death of another in violation of the rules of war, in reprisal for the actions of others, or because of that person's race, nationality, or political beliefs. The mere fact of membership in the SS,[5] the Gestapo, or similar Nazi organizations made an individual liable for service in Labor Battalions engaged in reconstruction work outside of Germany. The rhetoric of the New Deal made a tentative appearance in a clause calling for the elimination of all Junker[6] land holdings and their division among the peasantry, and Germans were strictly forbidden to attempt to escape the consequences of their sins by emigrating to other lands.

Taken as a whole, the Morgenthau Plan was a design for a radical reconstruction of Germany. Imbued with the belief of many New Dealers in the efficacy of grand plans as the solution to problems, it called for a total change in the occupations and life-styles of most Germans. The plan had two major premises: that all the German people and not just the Nazis deserved punishment for their crimes against humanity, and that an entire nation could be restructured and redirected by outside agents.[7] The arguments advanced by Morgenthau that Europe did not need German industry, that Britain would benefit from the elimination of German industrial competition, that the Germans could feed themselves without having to buy food from other countries, and that a hard policy toward Germany would help to maintain Soviet-American cooperation, all came after the fact. Punishment and reform lay at the heart of the Morgenthau Plan for Germany. Convinced of the underlying goodness of the common people in general, Morgenthau (and Roosevelt) believed that militarism and Nazi ideology had permanently tainted three generations of Germans. In essence, Morgenthau proposed returning the Germans to their primeval agrarian origins to start all over again.

Persuading the President

With the bureaucratic battle joined, Morgenthau pulled out all the stops in his efforts to get Roosevelt to decide once and for all on deindustrialization, as well as the issues of denazification and dismemberment. Using his close personal friendship with the president to good advantage, Morgenthau met with him repeatedly in late August and early September and enlisted the support of Eleanor Roosevelt and Harry Hopkins. At every opportunity the secretary played upon Roosevelt's disgust for Naziism, his desire to see the German people punished, and his increasingly strong belief that the elimination of German industry would improve Britain's foreign trade and help prevent her economic collapse. In spite of the president's preference for vague discussions and generalities, Morgenthau succeeded. At a meeting with the cabinet committee designated to discuss the German question—

Morgenthau, Stimson, Hull, and Hopkins were the members—Roosevelt flatly and unequivocally supported a hard-line policy. Reading from a summary of the Morgenthau Plan, Roosevelt quoted the line which denied that Europe needed a strong industrial Germany (see Documents 16 and 17). After commenting that most others disagreed with that statement, Roosevelt flatly endorsed it, adding that he favored the creation of an agricultural Germany.

The major opposition to the Morgenthau Plan came from Secretary of War Henry Stimson. Stimson's objections, summarized in a memorandum to the president dated September 9, 1944, challenged the very premises upon which the Morgenthau Plan rested (see Document 18). He carefully distinguished between Nazis and/or militarists as opposed to the mass of German people who had no choice but to obey. He scoffed at the notion that any outside force could successfully transmute an industrialized, complex society into a peaceful, contented, pastoral land devoid of any strong sense of nationalism. Echoing the arguments of John Maynard Keynes two decades earlier regarding the so-called Carthaginian Peace following World War I, Stimson predicted that such harsh measures would generate resentment and war rather than peaceful acceptance. He warned that, just as had happened after World War I, excessive severity would engender sympathy for the Germans and, moreover, that Europe did need the industrial output of Germany in order to rebuild and maintain economic prosperity. Secretary Hull, ill and primarily concerned with personal questions of his status rather than with the implementation of his policies, temporarily supported Morgenthau's economic proposals. Harry Hopkins, eager to become the high commissioner of the American zone in occupied Germany, cautiously agreed with the president, leaving Stimson alone in his attempt to sway Roosevelt. The president expressed some doubts about destroying all of the Ruhr's vast industry. Nevertheless, only two days before the start of the Quebec Conference with Churchill on September 11, Roosevelt had firmly endorsed the creation of an agricultural Germany.

State Department officials, aware of the president's sympathy for the Morgenthau Plan, prepared a memorandum for Hull which on the surface went a long way toward the sort of bureaucratic concensus Roosevelt usually favored. But careful reading made it clear that the State Department had not compromised at all. The position that Germany's economy should not dominate Europe or be reconvertible to wartime production still allowed the preservation of its industry. All references to communications and education referred to the elimination of Nazi influence, not to the complete reform of German society; and the memo recommended that the questions of partition and reparations be postponed until British and Soviet policies became clear. State Department officials, far more interested in the politico-economic role of Germany vis à vis the Soviet Union and in multilateralism—the search for an expansion of America's system of liberal capitalism—could never quite bring themselves to look at Germany as an enemy deserving of punishment. Some, like George Kennan, even opposed denazification programs, since that would eliminate the people upon whom Germany had to depend for leadership. Hoping that mere military defeat would convince Germany of the futility of aggression, Kennan claimed that denazification would only promote disharmony and that attempts to eliminate German nationalism were foredoomed to failure. Moreover, as Kennan later put it, "to my mind a sensible policy toward Germany was the first requirement of a sound postwar policy with relation to the Soviet Union itself. . . ."[8]

In spite of Stimson's belief, stated in his memoirs, that Roosevelt had not made any decision on postwar policy toward Germany before arriving in Quebec, American policy guidelines had been drawn. Stimson later insinuated that the president's health had affected his attitude toward Germany, but that ignores the thrust of Roosevelt's thinking toward the Germans since the start of the war. FDR's tired and wan physical appearance and his increasingly frequent lapses of memory, both symptoms which Morgenthau and Stimson noted, probably stemmed from his cardio-vascular illness, but his poor health does not change his earlier condemnations of German society in general. Like Morgenthau, Roosevelt rarely referred to the Nazis in his public and private remarks, preferring to encompass all Germans in his condemnations of war crimes and atrocities.

That attitude, consistently held since the outbreak of the war, shaped much of Roosevelt's basic policy toward Germany. In spite of other alternatives offered at various times, he advocated a stern denazification policy which included extensive reeducation programs; he supported the dismemberment of Germany into a number of independent states, all presumably constitutional democracies; he demanded the full demilitarization of Germany, both physically and socially and never seriously considered the arguments that Germany should serve as a buffer against the Soviet Union; and, after a short but intensive struggle within the bureaucracy, he firmly sided with Morgenthau's proposals for the complete deindustrialization of Germany. Like White and others in the Treasury Department, Roosevelt appeared dubious about trying to destroy totally the Ruhr industrial complex, but he clearly approved of the overarching goal of the Morgenthau Plan—the reordering of German society through increased, if not total, pastoralization.

The Quebec Conference offered an opportunity to wrap up the package. Although the British did not know it, Roosevelt had already indicated a willingness to accept the southern zone in Germany, which was the only loose end left regarding the zonal boundaries worked out by the EAC. Reparations, another problem which had been postponed because the EAC found itself unable to obtain firm policy guidelines from any of the three powers, were limited and defined by the Morgenthau Plan to immediate short-term payments based on dismantled industry. Long-term reparations would have required rehabilitation of the industrial plant and hence were forbidden. No one denied the legitimate claims of the Russians to substantial aid in order to rebuild their country, but such needs seemed likely to be satisfied more by an extension of American credits rather than by reparations.

Thus, as Roosevelt left to meet Prime Minister Churchill in Quebec City, he could assume that the question of postwar Germany no longer posed any great problem. He had reached a policy decision at home, an apparently workable plan existed, the Soviet Union had long favored a harsh peace, and Morgenthau's report of his talks with British Foreign Minister Eden indicated general British support for a program aimed at reforming as well as punishing the Germans. It was a classic example of the Roosevelt style: a vague consensus achieved by virtually ignoring arguments which did not appeal to him—but he retained full freedom of action to shift as he chose, since no formal policy statement yet existed.

Notes

1. Morgenthau, Memo of a Conference at Red Rice, Andover, England, August 15, 1944, Harry Dexter White Papers, Box 7, Princeton University Library, Princeton, N.J.

2. The Works Progress Administration, Civilian Conservation Corps, and Public Works Administration—all New Deal programs to provide relief during the Depression.

3. Adolf Hitler labeled the Versailles Treaty a *diktat;* meaning a harsh, imposed settlement into which the Germans had no input.

4. Presidential Diary, Aug. 25, 1944, p. 1391, Henry Morgenthau, Jr. papers, Franklin D. Roosevelt Library, Hyde Park, N.Y.

5. The SS were the Storm Troopers—the Nazi elite politico-military force.

6. The Junkers were the Prussian land-owning nobility which resided primarily in East Prussia, now part of Poland and the USSR, and Brandenburg/Prussia, now part of East Germany.

7. The notion of restructuring also characterized General Douglas MacArthur's administration of Japan after World War II, though in that case the changes were limited largely to the overt political structure, not the economy or society. His attempt to break up the large industrial oligopolies *(zaibatsu)* proved short-lived.

8. George F. Kennan, *Memoirs, 1925-1950* (Boston: Little, Brown, & Co., 1967), p. 175.

4

The Morgenthau Plan: Accepted or Rejected?

Back to Quebec

British leaders approached the second Quebec Conference, code named OCTAGON, with forebodings. With the war against Germany going well, postwar questions became more pressing, for the nature of American answers to British queries would play a major role in determining Britain's political and economic future. Because of their general agreement on military strategy and Roosevelt's policy of avoiding postwar decisions, the Americans had stalled in arranging the meeting, but Churchill understood that postwar problems could no longer wait.

As ever, the key postwar question was money, though it was raised largely in the form of a request for an extension of Lend-Lease, the vast American foreign aid program during the war. The problem of Germany, more urgent than ever because of Allied military advances, also demanded attention, and the British expected to discuss it during the talks. Even though no intrinsic relationship existed between American economic assistance to Britain and policy regarding postwar Germany, events indicate that during the Quebec Conference the resolution of one affected the resolution of the other. Both Roosevelt and Churchill felt deep concern over the economic plight of Great Britain and hoped to prevent that nation's collapse. Morgenthau, more concerned about the German question but still officially the president's advisor on postwar financial conditions in England, had seen the possibilities of connecting the destruction of German industry to the expansion of British industrial export markets and had regularly suggested that possibility to Roosevelt.

British Foreign Office predictions of the thrust of the upcoming Quebec Conference picked up that new equation once they received reports of the Morgenthau Plan. The British ambassador in Washington, Lord Halifax, informed his government of the new proposal for Germany as well as of the arguments presented pro and con within the American bureaucracy. Conversations with various American officials, among them Assistant Secretary of War John McCloy and presidential advisor Hopkins, brought out the idea that the deindustrialization of Germany could mean the reindustrialization of Britain. British diplomats remained dubious. One commented that the Americans "may be toying with the idea of supporting our economy at the expense of Germany's" and that "if they intend to put forward proposals of this kind we may have some exceedingly embarrassing moments with the

European Allies," and others in the Foreign Office suspected the Americans of trying to find a way out of the domestic political dilemma which any postwar aid-to-Britain program would inevitably stir up.[1] Even so, they warned Churchill and his advisors to be prepared to discuss such issues at the Quebec Conference even if Hopkins claimed that postwar Lend-Lease aid would not come up for formal discussion.

Halifax's reports also noted a lessening of support for a partition of Germany beyond detaching East Prussia and the restoring of Alsace-Lorraine to France (see Document 19). American reasoning, as related by Hopkins was that such partitioning would require prolonged occupation with a number of bad side effects, particularly too much fraternization. As someone noted on the cover of one draft of the Morgenthau Plan, "Every German girl who gets married means an American girl who does not."[2] Although Hopkins claimed to speak only for himself, he tended to believe that the Allies could best achieve security against Germany, while avoiding long-term occupation, through economic measures. Whether that required internationalization of the Ruhr, removal of German industry to Britain and Belgium, or some other steps remained unsettled; the point was that Churchill had best be prepared to discuss the issue during his upcoming talks with Roosevelt. Internal position papers prepared by various British Foreign Office officials indicated a consensus against dismemberment and in favor of the decentralization of Germany. Foreign Secretary Eden minuted his agreement to that concept, but suggested that the internationalization of the Ruhr and Rhineland could provide the best protection against German aggression. Like the French, Eden saw international sanctions against Germany as the only way to involve the United States permanently in the preservation of European security.

The question of Russia invariably cropped up in British internal policy discussions. Prophetically, dismemberment appeared to the British Chiefs of Staff[3] as the best guarantee against a Russo-German coalition and even offered the possibility of bringing southern Germany into some sort of entente with western Europe. But British Foreign Office officials remained uncertain of Soviet intentions regarding Germany (see Document 20). Fearing that support for a united Germany might ignite Russian fears of just such an anti-Soviet bloc, Eden and others flatly opposed such arguments as destructive of existing "high policy," namely the preservation of the wartime alliance between Britain and the Soviet Union. If Britain's policy toward Germany ever became a function of Cold War tension, such was not the case in the Fall of 1944.

Although Eden and the British Foreign Office obviously knew of the Morgenthau Plan about ten days before the Quebec Conference convened on September 11, 1944, Churchill apparently did not. Memoranda about the problem of postwar Germany uncharacteristically do not have any Churchill minutes attached, and one long paper intended for extensive circulation within the War Cabinet before the Quebec meeting seems to have gotten lost in the bureaucracy until later in September. Whatever the reason, when the

Morgenthau Plan came up during the talks, Churchill did not respond with the arguments favored by the Foreign Office. Unlike Morgenthau and even Roosevelt, the prime minister had no positive proposal to make. The initiative lay with the Americans.

At the outset of the Quebec talks, a number of issues relating to Germany lay awaiting joint policy decisions. One appealing aspect of the Morgenthau Plan was that it offered or at least indicated solutions to all of those hang-fire problems. The complete deindustrialization of Germany provided physical security against future German aggression by eliminating that nation's military capabilities. Both deindustrialization and denazification presaged an overall reform of German society and culture—a reform which would eventually permit Germany to reenter the community of nations. Dismemberment, made easier and economically feasible after deindustrialization, would further inhibit any redevelopment of German power or ultranationalism. The French and the Russians would receive some sort of territorial compensation and short-term reparations in kind would meet the immediate reconstruction needs of the Allies. With the quick and long-term elimination of any German threat, the need for a prolonged occupation dissipated, thus permitting the United States to accept the southern zone without fear of becoming entangled in any sort of guardianship over France. In the context of grand strategy, Roosevelt believed that the Russians preferred a drastic program for Germany; hence the Morgenthau Plan fit his overall hopes of postwar cooperation.

No one presented real alternative policies for Roosevelt to choose from at Quebec. Churchill's response was negative and offered no alternatives, and the prime minister himself squelched Eden's attempts to enter the discussions. Roosevelt did not bring Secretary of State Hull or any other important State Department official to the conference, giving Morgenthau a clear field to influence policy. Although the American military leaders attended, only Admiral William Leahy, the president's military advisor, regularly discussed nonmilitary matters, and even he was not present at the important discussion regarding Germany. Moreover, military interest centered on the question of assignment of occupation zones, and on the second day of the OCTAGON Conference the Combined Chiefs of Staff requested that the two heads of state resolve the question and issue some sort of guidance.

Alternative 1 Accepted: Churchill and Roosevelt Approve the Morgenthau Plan for Germany

On September 19, 1944, Churchill and Roosevelt initialed the memorandum which called for the conversion of Germany into a nation essentially pastoral and agricultural in nature (*Alternative 1:* see Document 1). This came about as the result of intensive discussions during the Quebec Conference. In those discussions, the full meaning and purposes of the Churchill-Roosevelt decision were made clear.

On the second day of the conference, after he had hinted to Churchill about the economic benefits which would accrue to Great Britain following the destruction of Germany's industry, Roosevelt cabled Morgenthau to come immediately to Quebec, primarily, as he later told Churchill, to discuss Germany. The next afternoon, September 13, the president told Morgenthau that Churchill had appeared excited about British domination of Europe's steel industry. He suggested that the Treasury Secretary talk to Churchill's close personal advisor, Lord Cherwell (the British paymaster-general). Roosevelt interpreted Churchill's remarks as favoring the sort of harsh peace proposed by Morgenthau, and believed 'that the prime minister intended to be tough.

That prediction contradicted the impressions Morgenthau had gleaned during his trip to England, a few weeks earlier, and at dinner that evening the secretary's previous information seemed vindicated. When, at Roosevelt and Cherwell's suggestion, Morgenthau outlined his plan for Germany, Churchill responded with annoyance and contempt. Claiming he did not want to chain himself to a dead German, the prime minister labeled the entire plan as "unnatural, unchristian and unnecessary."[4] Morgenthau denied that his program would starve the Germans, but Churchill remained dubious. Moreover, in spite of his earlier interest, he dismissed as insignificant the benefits which the destruction of German industry would provide for Britain. Perhaps the prime minister was playing devil's advocate, but whatever his motives, his reception to the plan gave Morgenthau a sleepless night.

Morgenthau's most effective ally was Lord Cherwell. A scientist and long-time supporter of Churchill, "the Prof." (as Churchill called him) could invariably gain the prime minister's attention. Adept at boiling scientific and statistical problems down to essentials, Cherwell put those talents to work in analyzing the Morgenthau Plan. Keenly aware of Churchill's overpowering worries about Britain's postwar economic situation, Cherwell claimed that the American proposal offered Britain a chance to stay out of bankruptcy by eliminating German competition. In addition, why should not Germany instead of Britain assume the burden of postwar suffering? Churchill may have been toying with the old notion of Germany as a barrier between Soviet Russia and the English Channel, but he obviously had not yet decided to break so sharply with the postwar cooperation policy advocated by Roosevelt and British Foreign Minister Anthony Eden. Given Morgenthau's claim that his plan had the support of Secretary of State Hull, and obviously unaware of the Foreign Office correspondence which indicated a sharp disagreement within the American government on the German question, Churchill had little reason to stand alone in favor of what seemed in comparison a "soft" policy toward Germany. There were other, more important questions which awaited decisions, particularly agreement on American financial aid to Britain. There was no sense in antagonizing Roosevelt on an issue which he apparently had decided. Whether those thoughts consciously occurred to Churchill is not known, but throughout the war the prime minister had usually followed a policy of carefully selecting only the most important issues when he decided to disagree openly with Roosevelt. Aware of America's overwhelming power and traditional go-it-alone tendencies, Churchill avoided direct confrontations when he could. His anger over disagreements concerning military action in the Mediterranean, for example, related to Britain's postwar strategic position; harsh treatment of the Germans hardly seemed of comparable magnitude. Given Lord Cherwell's assurances of the Morgenthau Plan's practicality, Churchill had no real argument against the proposal.

By the day after Churchill's first exposure to the Morgenthau Plan, the prime minister had made a one-hundred-eighty degree change in his position. Historians have tended to interpret that change as related to Churchill's desire to obtain an agreement on postwar Lend-Lease aid to Britain. That is possible although there is no indication in any of the extant records or memoirs of such a direct connection. Morgenthau later denied that such was the case, although Churchill did hint at it in his memoirs. If true, then there is some irony in the relationship, for the strongest practical argument for the Morgenthau Plan as far as Roosevelt was concerned was that it would aid Britain. Although the Treasury Department proposal solved many other problems, Roosevelt's concern about Britain's possible economic collapse clearly provided Morgenthau with his major weapon against counterproposals from the State and War departments. Just as in 1940 and 1941, once convinced of Britain's real need, Roosevelt became determined to provide the necessary economic assistance. In fact, Morgenthau later claimed that, had it not been for his interference, Roosevelt would have made a more extensive commitment to almost unconditional postwar Lend-Lease, in spite of extensive State Department plans to use such promised aid as a lever against various restrictive British economic practices. It seems likely that at Quebec, Roosevelt would have supported postwar aid to Britain regardless of Churchill's position on the Morgenthau Plan. If Churchill assumed that Roosevelt had elevated the Morgenthau Plan to the level of vital policy, then the irony deepens. Roosevelt had opted for the plan, but only verbally and at least partly because Morgenthau had told him that Eden and Hull also favored such harsh treatment of Germany. In his memoirs, Churchill casually dismissed his acceptance of the Morgenthau Plan as something done in haste. His physician and occasional confidant, Lord Moran, thought otherwise. Claiming that Churchill refused to admit his mistake, Moran believed that Cherwell convinced the prime minister that the Morgenthau Plan should receive Britain's support.

Whatever the reasons, on September 14 Churchill not only endorsed the plan but complained that Cherwell's presentation, carefully toned down in order to gain the prime minister's approval, was too soft on Germany. When Cherwell met with Morgenthau to discuss a draft memorandum of the previous day's consensus on Germany, the secretary expressed similar dissatisfaction with the relatively gentle tone. Noting that the prime minister had mused about changing Germany into a nineteenth-century agricultural nation, Morgenthau suggested that they again discuss the proposal and then rewrite the official memorandum.

Their meeting that afternoon included Roosevelt, Churchill, Morgenthau, Cherwell, and Eden, who had just arrived from London. After signing the joint memorandum which provided for the continuance of Lend-Lease to Britain after the defeat of Germany and until the end of the war against Japan, Churchill asked for Cherwell's draft memo on planning for Germany. When Morgenthau explained that the Cherwell memorandum made too weak a case, Churchill eventually ended up dictating one of his own, using as a rough draft an outline which Morgenthau had prepared (*Alternative 1:* see Document 21). Roosevelt's only contribution, other than an occasional wisecrack, was the insertion of the phrase "in Germany" following the mention of those industries which could be easily converted from peacetime to wartime production. Taken in conjunction with the closing statement which referred to the pastoralization of Germany, that phrase indicated that the memorandum concerned all Germany, not just the Saar and Ruhr industrial areas (see Document 1). A comparison of Morgenthau's draft and the memo as dictated by Churchill demonstrates that, once converted to the Morgenthau Plan, the prime minister seemed willing to pull out all the stops.

As Morgenthau later pointed out, the word "pastoral" came from Churchill, not the Treasury Department. The only objections came, to Morgenthau's surprise, from Anthony Eden. Though Eden did not advocate the creation of a German buffer state against Russia, as some British officials did, he also believed that the Allies would never have the perseverance actually to make the Morgenthau Plan work. Unlike Roosevelt, who saw the plan as an easy, workable solution which would permit a relatively quick American withdrawal from Europe, Eden never swayed from his conviction that the destruction of German industry and the internationalization of the industrial areas would demand an even greater commitment. Morgenthau, unused to the careful phrasing used by diplomats who hope to avoid giving offense, never noticed that Eden had always qualified his vague comments about Morgenthau's overall proposals. Churchill, obviously annoyed and embarrassed by Eden's objections, instructed the foreign minister not to bring up the subject with the War Cabinet. Rejecting Eden's claim that the Morgenthau Plan went against a number of statements and plans already made, the prime minister used Cherwell's argument; everything boiled down to a question of who would get the export trade and, given the choice between the German and the English people, the decision was obvious. A cable from the British War Cabinet, initiated by Eden, arrived on the following day. It echoed Eden's objections and presaged future British policy, but it came too late to prevent Churchill's approval of the memorandum (see Document 22).

Ironically, Churchill's decision was more of a snap judgment than that of the supposedly haphazard and impulsive Roosevelt. Convinced by Cherwell and happy to take a harsh line with Britain's enemy, Churchill made a potentially momentous decision with little or no reflection. Roosevelt had, at least, considered various elements underlying the Morgenthau Plan for much of the war. Although the ink was scarcely dry on the actual document, the notions of deindustrialization, denazification, and dismemberment had long been in his mind. Similar proposals had appeared in England, offered by Lord Vansittart and others, but Churchill apparently never gave them any thought.

Not surprisingly, agreement on the nagging problem of occupation zones quickly followed. That same afternoon, Roosevelt agreed to take the southern zone of Germany in return for American lines of communication which did not pass through France; a commitment which eventually translated into American control of two German ports on the North Sea, Bremen and Bremerhaven. Roosevelt later told Morgenthau that he had purposefully delayed on that issue until he found Churchill in a good humor following settlement of all the other issues, but there was more to Roosevelt's decision than mere tactics. Although he had indicated even before the Quebec talks that the zonal question did not pose any real problems, the Morgenthau Plan promised a speedy way out of Europe and, more to the point, out of any involvement in the chaos and revolution which threatened to engulf France. Possibly even more important, such zonal assignments meant that the British had to occupy and carry out the Morgenthau Plan in the two most industrialized areas—the Ruhr and the Saar. British willingness to deal with the problem of occupying Austria also may have made the southern zone more palatable to Roosevelt.

Campaign Against the Plan

At the very moment of Morgenthau's triumph, his opponents in Washington were planning the defeat of the Treasury Department's plan. At the instigation of James F. Byrnes, Roosevelt's advisor and general trouble-shooter, *New York Times* columnist Arthur Krock telephoned Secretary of State Hull to inform him that Morgenthau had rushed off to Quebec—to a conference where only military and economic questions appeared on the preconference agenda. Obviously the Morgenthau Plan for Germany would be discussed. Stimson, fearing such discussions, had talked with British Ambassador Lord Halifax and suggested that Churchill and Roosevelt be advised to refer any questions regarding the control of Germany's postwar economy to a small *ad hoc* committee. The advice was sent to Churchill at Quebec, but obviously had little impact.

Shortly after he and Churchill had initialed the memo on postwar Germany, Roosevelt cabled Secretary Hull the text of the agreement. The president's transmittal remarks indicated that he assumed Hull would approve, but he failed to consider Hull's long-standing pique over Morgenthau's influence in what the secretary of state considered his province. In spite of previous promises, Roosevelt had once again made foreign policy without consulting Hull or other State Department spokesmen, and the secretary's anger rose. Even though he had already given virtual command of the department to his eventual successor, Edward Stettinius, Hull decided to fight the issue. Though it is hard to say whether the substance or the behind-the-back approval of the Morgenthau Plan most concerned him, Hull reversed his earlier tacit approval and came out strongly against the program.

The strongest and eventually most effective opposition to the Morgenthau Plan came from Secretary of War Henry Stimson. Even though the Quebec memorandum included only a small portion of the full Morgenthau Plan, Stimson realized that the broad philosophy had received approval and that implementation would follow.

The main reason for the success of Stimson and his assistant secretary, John McCloy, who took control of the German debate from his old and weary boss, was that the War Department accepted major portions of the Morgenthau Plan, in both spirit and fact. Stimson's most eloquent critique of the Morgenthau Plan challenged only the pastoralization program—nothing else. Granted, the Treasury Department saw that aspect of the plan as integral to the hoped for reforms, but the domestic New Deal had never actually adopted long-term reform of such a nature, planned and implemented by government, and no one even suggested that such arguments would carry any weight with the president. Although Stimson seemingly endorsed Hull's overall economic program when he labeled the elimination of German competition in order to benefit Great Britian as the "shortsighted cupidity of the victors and the negation of all that Secretary Hull has been trying to accomplish since 1933," his real argument was that forcing such a revolutionary change on the German people violated fundamental rights— freedom and the pursuit of happiness (*Alternative 2:* see Document 23). The concern of generals Marshall and Eisenhower for law, order, and efficient military government meant that the War Department also opposed some of the harsher political measures espoused by Morgenthau. Still, both departments agreed on punishment for war criminals, the elimination of heavy industry related to war-making capabilities, total and complete demilitarization, extremely limited and short-term reparations, the break up of the Junker estates, and the partitioning of Germany—including the internationalization of the Saar and the Ruhr—once military occupation ended. Treasury officials were well aware that any delay in such things as partitioning only made them more difficult and hence less likely, but there is no indication that such delays were part of some sort of crafty plan on the part of the War Department. Stimson's sense of moral outrage appears quite geniune, and the War Department had always avoided involvement in long-term planning for Germany.

Roosevelt's endorsement of the Morgenthau Plan flowed from many factors, among them his very emotional dislike of the Germans and his belief that the plan could command general support in his cabinet and hence among the American public. The Stimson-McCloy approach still called for punishment and reeducation of the Germans, and Hull's shift from ambiguity to opposition toward the Morgenthau Plan meant that Roosevelt had a major dispute on his hands.

As befits any American decision in America, particularly one by Roosevelt, domestic politics probably tipped the balance. In spite of widespread predictions that he would easily win reelection to a fourth term—with the two-term tradition safely out of the way—the politician inside Roosevelt never took anything for granted (at least not since the Supreme Court "packing" fight and subsequent congressional elections defeat in 1938). Hull's appointment had originally stemmed almost exclusively from his domestic political power base, not his proposals in international affairs almost exclusively—hence Roosevelt's frequent use of others in government to make foreign policy. That had not changed by 1944, and the president did not want a public disagreement with Hull just before the election.

Someone, probably James Byrnes, understood the pressures working on Roosevelt and in true Washington fashion enlisted the aid of the press. On September 21, investigative reporter Drew Pearson broke the story of the division in the cabinet over the Army Handbook for Germany. Arthur Krock, a friend and political ally of both Byrnes and Hull, followed the next day with a column in the *New York Times* about Morgenthau's trip to Quebec, bemoaning such bypassing of the secretary of state. On September 23 the *Wall Street Journal* published a fairly accurate summary of the Morgenthau Plan, including a statement that the proposal would force thirty million Germans to move elsewhere, thus further weakening Germany's ability to wage war. By every account, including British embassy press summaries sent regularly to London, overall press opinion of the Morgenthau Plan was unfavorable.

As the campaign against the plan reached a crescendo, Roosevelt began to back off. When Morgenthau attempted, on September 29, to drop in at the White House to discuss the newspaper reaction, Roosevelt uncharacteristically refused to see him. Later that same day during a press conference, one of the president's favorite forums for disclosing his decisions (even before telling his cabinet), Roosevelt flatly denied that a split had developed in his cabinet over the question of postwar Germany. The president, dissembling, made no reference to the Cabinet Committee on Germany, the formal location of the dispute. Moreover, he also made public his letter to the head of the Foreign Economic Administration, Leo Crowley, containing instructions for Crowley to work out policies regarding Germany's postwar economy, particularly with regard to exports and future foreign trade. Even to mention such notions was an almost direct repudiation of the Morgenthau Plan.

At the same time, Hull and Stimson redoubled their efforts to get the president to back away from the Quebec memorandum. Hull tried to give Roosevelt an easy way out by suggesting that the entire question be referred to the European Advisory Commission, and commented in his published memoirs (which are, it must be said, notoriously unreliable) that the president merely replied that he had not committed himself to the Morgenthau Plan. Roosevelt's decision the next day (September 26, 1944) to abolish the special Cabinet Committee on Germany indicated his desire to squelch the controversy, and on the following day he retreated even further. Telling Stimson that his intention had not ever been to turn Germany into an agricultural nation, Roosevelt claimed his real motive was to prevent an economic collapse in Britain. That was, of course, only a half-truth. Roosevelt had seized upon the Morgenthau Plan partly as a means of aiding Britain's postwar economy, but he had also accepted and made specific contributions to that portion of the program which called for social reform. As ever, there was a problem with words, Churchill's phrase, pastoralization, brought on visions of the total destruction of every element of German industry; but even the harshest version of the Morgenthau Plan called only for the elimination of heavy industry, not those related to services and basic consumer goods. Stimson chose to take the extreme meaning, while Roosevelt always viewed the Quebec memorandum as a statement of general purpose rather than fixed policy.

Decision by Bureaucracy

Roosevelt's reaction when cornered in a bureaucratic, political, or diplomatic dispute was almost invariably to procrastinate, usually by either promising all things to all parties or by openly putting off any decision. He could not always threaten to lock the disputants in a room until they reached agreement (a technique he did use once with his cabinet), so he frequently tried to achieve consensus by postponement, assuming that eventually one side or the other would weary of the fight. So it was with postwar planning for Germany. With the failure in late September of the daring airborne assault on Arnhem, the chance of a RANKIN situation in Germany seemed doubtful, and the president had what he liked the most—more time.

Since he could count on Morgenthau's loyalty and unflinching support, Roosevelt—with the election in mind—proceded to massage the injured feelings of Hull and Stimson. Obviously wishing to postpone a decision and not merely transfer the initiative from the Treasury to the State Department, he forcefully instructed Hull not to submit the question of Germany's postwar economy to the European Advisory Commission, but simultaneously commented that he did not intend to eradicate completely industry in the Ruhr and Saar. A few days later he disingenuously told Stimson that Morgenthau had "pulled a boner," and pretended shock and dismay at the very idea of totally eliminating the industrial plant in the Saar and Ruhr and converting Germany into a pastoral nation.[5] Roosevelt's deception apparently satisfied Stimson, who concluded that the Quebec memorandum was not a mature policy decision. He never again discussed the issue with the president.

Hull and those in the State Department who looked to Germany for both an economic and a political contribution to European stability were not so sure. Even before the president's first retreat from the Quebec memorandum, the State Department attempted to chip away at the overall concept of Morgenthau's plan (see Document 24). The alternatives offered by the department were subtle, but crucially different. After claiming that the State Department had never had its day in court on the German question, the memo used the vaguest of terms to recommend demilitarization, denazification, and controls (of an unspecified nature and for an unspecified purpose) over the German educational and communications systems. On the key items, partition and long-term economic objectives, the State Department recommended policies which differed radically from the Morgenthau Plan. It suggested that consideration of partition (as separated from such territorial adjustments as the return of Alsace-Lorraine) be deferred until Russia and Britain could be fully consulted, and it proposed that any economic planning aim only at preventing the development of war production and eliminating the supposed domination by Germany of the European economy. The State Department's primary goal—the creation of a world economy compatible with the American economic system—was reflected in a suggestion that German self-sufficiency be eliminated, but only to the point at which Germany became dependent upon world (American?) markets.

Roosevelt, in one of his last written responses to the debate, phrased a carefully ambiguous answer to Hull which mandated postponement of any real decision (see Document 25). Rather than choose among various unsatisfying alternatives, the president tried to hold the entire issue in abeyance. Again emphasizing the advisory nature of the EAC, Roosevelt expressed the fear that such bodies tended to carry out their own advice. Roosevelt knew that the EAC faithfully reflected State Department thinking, and his instructions demonstrate that the president did not want that department to set policy for postwar Germany. Nor was he ready to choose between the State and Treasury departments' concepts regarding the controversial question of deindustrialization. Although the president clearly endorsed those portions of Hull's memorandum which called for social and political reforms, Roosevelt carefully side-stepped Hull's suggestion that Germany be integrated into the overall world (American liberal capitalist) system by agreeing in principle, while expressing confusion about the meaning of some of the language used. Since agreement in principle is, to any politician, a nonbinding and virtually meaningless commitment, Roosevelt's answer effectively returned the bureaucratic battle over Germany back to square one—but only as it concerned the top level officials.

The cabinet-level struggle had degenerated into what the British called a "wearisome claptrap debate . . . undiminished in volume or in confusion over terms,"[6] but others more concerned with providing immediate occupation directions to SHAEF (Supreme Headquarters Allied Expeditionary Force; i.e., General Eisenhower's command) could still generate meaningful decisions, even if they were officially only interim instructions. In the wake of Roosevelt's order to withdraw the SHAEF "Handbook for Military Government of Germany," lesser officials working for the Cabinet Committee on Germany agreed early in September, 1944, that a draft of an interim directive for Germany should be drawn up and sent to Eisenhower. With the EAC bypassed and the Roosevelt cabinet unable to agree upon broad policy, the second-level bureaucrats took over.

The lines of negotiation at that level were still centered around the three basic alternatives offered back in 1943. The Treasury Department

representatives proposed the total economic, social, and political restructuring of Germany; the War Department people favored measures which
would effectively eliminate any chance of German military resurgence but
tended to shy away from any long-term responsibility for reforms; and
opposed any terms which could create long-lasting resentment or mitigate
against the relatively speedy integration of Germany into the world economy.
The fourth alternative, the use of Germany as a pawn in the creation of a new
cordon sanitaire against Soviet Russia, remained only a vague idea lurking in
the minds of a few American and British planners.

Treasury and War department suggestions for the temporary instructions
to Eisenhower differed primarily on the economic issues. Bargains were
suggested and struck over questions of denazification, punishment of war
criminals, and fraternization with the Germans, but when the War Department proposed merely giving the military authorities control over the
economy without any clear-cut policy guidance, the Treasury representatives
inserted guidelines which established positive direction. The Treasury hand
was strengthened by news of the Quebec memorandum on Germany, and
John McCloy, the primary War Department negotiator, finally settled for a
statement which specifically called for military control over the economy (as
opposed to the Treasury's suggestion of leaving the Germans to stew in their
own juices), but which included a strong statement prohibiting any steps
aimed at the rehabilitation of the German economy as a whole (see
Document 26).

State Department officials unalterably opposed any such restrictions,
but the Quebec memorandum left them little room in which to
maneuver. Angrily, the diplomats reported to Hull that Treasury officials
claimed Roosevelt had repudiated the State Department position and that
all further policy regarding Germany had to be cleared with the Treasury
Department. In a last ditch effort to prevent a bureaucratic *fait
accompli*, Hull approved the interim directive for Germany but added a
reservation in the form of a letter to Stimson (see Document 27).
Innocuous as the reservation appeared, it permitted the military commander in Germany to do whatever he wished if it related to the safety
or health of the occupying forces. It was only a short step from there to
a statement that the health of occupying forces requried that German
coal mines produce, that German industry provide support, and so on.
Both Morgenthau and McCloy interpreted Hull's letter as a face-saving
gesture, and the enthusiastic support given the draft of the interim
directive by Eisenhower's deputy, General Bedell Smith, confirmed the War
Department's position. Treasury Department fears were borne out two years
later, in 1946, when General Lucius Clay, American high commissioner in
Germany, utilized the authority granted the military to begin the rehabilitation of German industry. But as of October, 1944, an elated Morgenthau
believed that he had succeeded in getting the bureaucracy to implement his
plan, even if the president had developed second thoughts.

British Reactions

That was no small victory, since the draft of the interim directive, assigned the number JCS 1067 when circulated to the Joint Chiefs of Staff, became the American proposal for a Combined Chiefs of Staff[7] directive on Germany. To Morgenthau's dismay, the British refused to accept JCS 1067 as combined Anglo-American policy. Instead, late in October, the British government submitted its own proposed directive for Germany; a directive intended to establish long-term policy rather than merely deal with the more immediate postsurrender situation. The British document, ninety-seven pages of detailed directives to the future military commander in Germany, reflected the prevailing attitude in the British Foreign Office. Even McCloy complained that the British proposal appeared overly concerned with preserving the basic structure of German society, and the Treasury Department reacted even more strongly. In a memo which McCloy approved, Morgenthau castigated the British for violating almost every precept of the Morgenthau Plan, from placing too much emphasis upon economic rehabilitation to the suggestion of arming the German police with tanks and heavy weapons. McCloy suggested that the British document was the product of the old guard professionals in the Foreign Office, though he did not draw the logical conclusion that anti-Soviet attitudes might have played a role. Morgenthau asked if McCloy wished the Treasury critique to go via Lord Cherwell to Churchill as an unofficial joint Treasury-War departmental reaction, and McCloy readily agreed. It illustrates the nature of the bureaucratic struggle in Washington as well as McCloy's political slipperiness that the assistant secretary of war flatly lied to State Department officials by claiming that he had tried to talk Morgenthau out of giving the document to Cherwell. The War Department cared primarily about granting almost complete freedom of action to the occupation commander; the Treasury Department cared almost exclusively about the long-term implications of any decision. They could both agree that the British proposal was unacceptable, though for basically different reasons.

Actually, British policy-making regarding postwar Germany was almost as confused and contradictory as in the United States. And, as in the United States, the trail of confusion and uncertainty led directly back to the head of government. In spite of speculation by some Americans, including Harry Dexter White, that Churchill had endorsed the Quebec memorandum on Germany only in order to obtain a favorable agreement on Lend-Lease, the prime minister's commitment to deindustrialization and pastoralization for Germany was more than merely perfunctory. When he went to Moscow in mid-October, 1944, for the TOLSTOY conference with Stalin, Churchill clearly and enthusiastically presented the outline of the Quebec memorandum and the Morgenthau Plan. Asked by Russian Foreign Minister Vyacheslav Molotov for his opinion of the Morgenthau Plan, Churchill obliquely replied that he still opposed any mass execution of Germans after the war but believed "it was necessary to kill as many as possible in the field."[8] Stalin endorsed the concept of a hard peace and stated that German heavy industry would have to be reduced to a minimum. Obviously fearing a resurgence of German power, the Russian premier claimed that any chance of revenge had to be denied to Germany; harsh measures which prevented future war were, in that sense, the most humane. He and Churchill agreed that England should get the markets previously dominated by German exports and that Germany should not have a merchant fleet. They likewise agreed on plans to internationalize the Saar, Ruhr, and Kiel Canal areas, and also broached the question of a separate Rhineland state. A pleased Churchill, long a supporter of a Danubian federation, reported to Roosevelt that Stalin had changed his position and appeared willing to see Vienna as the capital of a south German state comprised of Austria, Bavaria, Wurttemberg, and Baden, though the discussions make Stalin's fears of an anti-Soviet entente very evident. Stalin's motives are never clear, but in this case he appeared as concerned about a unified German state which could aid the West as British diplomats were about a unified German state siding with Russia. The two leaders were like two Cheshire cats; final exchange after the discussions on Germany and Europe epitomized their satisfaction at having reached a spheres of influence agreement by playing a sort of children's board game, using nations as the pieces:

> THE PRIME MINISTER thought that there was very little divergence of opinion between them. It was a pity that when God created the world he had not consulted them.
> MARSHAL STALIN said it was God's first mistake (see Document 28).

Unlike discussions about Germany's economy or socio-political makeup, talks about postwar partitioning clearly fell into two different phases: the immediate or interim period, and the permanent arrangements which would come with a final peace treaty. Moreover, partitioning did not refer to certain obvious boundary adjustments which all parties had agreed upon. It was firmly settled that Alsace and Lorraine were to go to France and East Prussia to Russia and Poland, that some sort of boundary adjustment between Germany and Poland would occur, and that the unification of Austria with Germany would end. The existence of a three-power agreement on zones of occupation effectively eliminated any need for quick agreement on plans for the permanent breakup of the German state once the boundary adjustments had taken place. In spite of later claims by Soviet historians that Stalin had never supported the breakup of Germany, Stalin's position at the Teheran Conference, at the Tolstoy Conference, and his discussions with Charles de Gaulle in Moscow in early December, demonstrated his preference for a permanently partitioned Germany.[9]

The Foreign Office quickly expressed opposition to Churchill's statements to Stalin. It claimed that dismemberment was impractical and that deindustrialization meant the end of any chance of gaining reparations as well as being injurious to general European economic health. The first indication of Churchill's move away from the economic aspects of the Morgenthau Plan came in an exchange of telegrams with his old friend and advisor, Field Marshall Jan Smuts, prime minister of South Africa. Churchill had sent Smuts a copy of his report to Roosevelt after the Moscow Conference with Stalin. Smuts replied with a strong endorsement of partition for Germany, suggesting that an isolated Prussia might depend upon Britain for security just as Prussia had during the Napoleonic Wars. Fearful of Russian expansion, Smuts advised against giving Poland sizeable portions of German territory, since Poland appeared destined to become a Russian satellite. He agreed that German crimes deserved punishment, but asserted that they were a great people who should be integrated into the European community, for "a ruined and poisoned Germany spells a frustrated Europe."[10] Churchill's response defended the transfer of territory to Poland and explained that moving the Germans out of such territories should prevent future problems. He ignored the warning about Soviet expansion but agreed with Smuts that the Germans ought to have a "reasonable means of life."[11]

In spite of Churchill's wavering, Foreign Office memoranda steadily advised that the British government oppose the economic portions of the Morgenthau Plan, particularly those which called for drastic deindustrialization and those which would permit unabated inflation. Noting that Eden had repeatedly stated publicly that he opposed letting Germany become a trouble spot which could infect all Europe, the Foreign Office supported various forms of partitioning and decentralization, but expressed grave doubts about draconian economic measures which would only create chaos and bitterness. In a long report printed in late December, 1944, the Armistice and Post-War Committee in the Foreign Office concluded that none of the basic tenets of the Morgenthau Plan had any validity (see Document 29). The report claimed that turning Germany into an agrarian nation was not the most effective means of providing security against future German aggression; that there would be little or no economic benefits accruing to Britain because of deindustrialization; and that the Morgenthau Plan would create economic havoc in the Ruhr and Saar, the areas Britain would have to administer (a fact Roosevelt understood when he finally accepted the southern zone).

Thus, as preparations began for the meeting of Churchill, Roosevelt, and Stalin at Yalta, the British government had begun to reach some sort of agreement on opposing the Morgenthau Plan. Kept abreast of the debate within the American government, Churchill apparently began to slide back to his pre-Quebec position. The only reference to postwar planning for Germany in the many Churchill-Roosevelt exchanges which crossed the Atlantic between October, 1944, and February, 1945, was a cryptic message drafted by the president which clearly indicated Roosevelt's belief in the eventual redevelopment of the German economy. Sent to Churchill's following news of the sinking of the German battleship *Tirpitz*, the message read:

> The death of the TIRPITZ is great news. We must help the Germans by never letting them build anything like it again, thus putting the German Treasury on its feet.[12]

Official policy still called for disarmament, but deindustrialization seemed less certain.

Bickering between the State and Treasury departments over basic policy toward Germany continued during the months before the Yalta Conference. As the same time, the War Department continually put forth suggestions for small revisions to JCS 1067, though the thrust of those revisions was in the direction of lessening restrictions on the authority of military government, including its power to impose economic restrictions. Although the president toyed with the State Department and its new secretary, Edward Stettinius, he refused either to repudiate the Morgenthau Plan or endorse any specific long-term policy for Germany. In spite of repeated meetings, exchanges of memoranda, and the good personal relationship between Morgenthau and Stettinius (as opposed to Hull's open resentment at Morgenthau's role in foreign policy), nothing changed. Whenever any agency proposed a lessening of the harsh peace Morgenthau proposed, his staff argued against it. Treasury officials used their clear authority over financial matters to insure that the Germans retained full responsibility for their fiscal and related economic affairs, lest conscientious army authorities conclude that they had the duty to maintain the German monetary system. Morgenthau became increasingly concerned about arguments that the Soviet Union's genuine need for reparations necessitated the rehabilitation of the German economy, and countered with a strong endorsement of a no-strings-attached ten billion dollar credit to Russia. Not only would that eliminate the need for long-term reparations, but it would, according to Morgenthau, cement Russo-American relations. Morgenthau detected within the State Department the rise of the argument that a strong Germany was needed in order to offset the Soviet Union, and he hoped to nip that notion in the bud.

The clearest statement of the State Department program came in a memorandum sent by Stettinius to Roosevelt in late November. Although officials in the department forwarded additional statements on the subject, this one succinctly summed up their proposed policy. It differentiated between immediate occupation policy, which should be severe, and long-term programs. Security against Germany could come only through an inter-national peace-keeping organization, and the paper flatly stated that Germany should eventually be integrated "into a liberal world economy" (*Alternative 3:* see Document 30). The president indicated his continued opposition to reparations, but never really answered the memo.

All Morgenthau's attempts to reinforce before the Yalta meeting, the president's fast-disappearing commitment to the Treasury Department's program met with a similar fate. Apparently aware that the British no longer believed in the economic benefits they would gain from the Morgenthau Plan, the secretary instead emphasized the need to guarantee security against the rebirth of German power and dropped a hint about the danger involved in trying to set up Germany as a buffer against communism and the Soviet Union (see Document 31). Even that attempt to appeal to Roosevelt's favorite policy—cooperation with the Russians—failed to gain a response.

The Alternatives—Still Open

Thus, on the eve of the Big Three meeting in the Crimea, Roosevelt had the same set of alternatives before him that had existed all along. He could reendorse the Morgenthau Plan for Germany; he could change direction sharply and adopt the State Department program for security through economic interdependence in a world economy which integrated the German industrial output into the broader picture; or he could make no decision which would be a choice of the third alternative—letting the War Department set policy with a relatively free hand. The fourth alternative, using Germany as a bulwark against Russia, would never be formally presented to Roosevelt.

It is one of the great peculiarities of history that lost causes should have dominated Anglo-American policy during the most critical and potentially promising of all the major wartime conferences—the meeting of Churchill, Roosevelt, and Stalin at Yalta in the Russian Crimea from February 2 through 11, 1945. Churchill, and to a lesser degree Roosevelt, attempted somehow to wrest Poland from the Russian embrace; State Department and Foreign Office officials had recognized this to be a lost cause back in the fall of 1944, although they often refused to admit it.[13] Eager to get the Soviet Union into the war against Japan, Roosevelt made concessions to Russian territorial demands in East Asia, but not until he obtained a modicum of support from Stalin for Chiang Kai-Shek's Chinese Nationalist government—another lost cause. The United Nations Organization, which the State Department and Stalin saw as the means to preserve world peace, though for obviously different reasons, similarly proved a lost cause. However, Germany and the far-reaching ramifications of the German question were anything but lost. A wide range of alternatives remained available to Roosevelt and the other leaders—choices which ultimately played a critical role in defining the nature and strategy of the Cold War.

Although no one spoke of such great power conflicts at the Yalta talks, only the Americans failed to view Germany from such a Cold War perspective. Roosevelt looked at dismemberment as a means of permanently relegating the divided Germanies to a position of impotence in international affairs; he saw deindustrialization as a way to aid the British economy; he preferred reparations in kind and for a short-term because he accepted Morgenthau's argument that long-term reparations from production would stimulate the kind of heavy industry which could compete with British exports and quickly convert to wartime production. He also had an intense aversion to any kind of postwar settlements which involved monetary obligations—a result of the unpleasant World War I war debts controversy. Roosevelt's long-standing support for a general spheres of influence arrangement following the war (i.e., the Four Policemen concept with Russia, Great Britain, the United States, and eventually, China, generally supervising affairs in their own geographic area, as well as his opposition to any permanent American entanglement in European political problems, mitigated against any thoughts of Russo-American confrontation in Germany. To be sure,

American planners, particularly in the State Department, expressed constant and increasing concern over the future role of the Soviet Union in Europe, but as long as Franklin Roosevelt remained active and in control, those fears never came to dominate American policy. Germany was a unique and separate problem, and Roosevelt hoped to insure that such a problem never arose again. At the same time, a solution to any major problem had to contribute to the cooperative postwar relationship between the great powers. For that relationship, even if disguised by the rhetoric and structure of a United Nations Organization, formed the crux of Roosevelt's hopes for peace in the postwar world. A prosperous Britain and a satisfied Russia outweighed any other considerations.

The third member of the Big Three, Stalin, arrived at Yalta with a somewhat distorted view of Anglo-American policy regarding Germany. Given the discussion with Churchill at Moscow four months earlier and the little to the contrary from the prime minister heard since then, the Russian had to assume that some form of deindustrialization would occur, along with harsh punishment for German war criminals, total and complete disarmament, and some kind of dismemberment. A hint of Churchill's desire to postpone any decision on partitioning, a policy he pursued successfully at Yalta, appeared in a message to Stalin in December, 1944, which suggested that firm decisions on dismemberment should await the negotiation of a formal peace treaty, though the issue could receive attention at the Yalta meeting.

Whether from health, habit, or a conscious tactic, Roosevelt played only a minor part in the Yalta discussions on Germany. The most detailed talks took place between the three foreign ministers—Eden, Molotov, and Stettinius. The Big Three leaders tended largely to ratify the recommendations coming out of those talks, although Churchill and Stalin did have particular axes to grind on certain issues. Churchill, increasingly fearful of the future power relationships in Europe, fought to prevent any final decision on dismemberment; Stalin, deeply concerned about rebuilding devastated Russia before that country's economic and industrial weakness became fully known to the western powers, concentrated upon obtaining extensive reparations.

Closely related to the Soviet demands for reparations was their request, made in January, 1945, for a large program of credits from the United States. Morgenthau, who advocated a ten billion dollar credit as a means of avoiding the need to rebuild German industry as well as a way to promote good Soviet-American relations, endorsed the concept. The State Department did not. Echoing the recommendations of the American ambassador to Russia, W. Averell Harriman, Stettinius and his subordinates argued that such credits should depend upon Soviet willingness to cooperate on political issues. In other words, American economic power would be more wisely used as a coercive agent rather than as a means of promoting trust and good will. Morgenthau and Stettinius had the same goal—the enhancement of American security by establishing economic relationships with the Soviet Union. Both programs assumed that such relationships would put Russia on the road to political, social, and economic reforms of a western style. No one spoke or wrote of the Soviet Union becoming a liberal capitalist state, but that clearly represented the ultimate goal of both State and Treasury departmental thinking. Roosevelt, uncertain about the effect of either approach, typically refused to choose between them. He never answered Harriman's steady stream of recommendations from Moscow, yet he told both Treasury and State department officials that he agreed with them. When Russian Foreign Minister Molotov broached the issue at Yalta, Stettinius stated that he would personally discuss such credits then, later in Moscow, or in Washington—but those discussions never took place.

Decisions at Yalta

The Russians were the strongest advocates of a firm commitment at Yalta to the breakup of the German state. When Churchill tried to evade the issue, Stalin summarized Anglo-American statements on the question. Eventually, after Roosevelt agreed that the principle, though not the program, for partitioning should be agreed upon, Stalin accepted a vague statement regarding the terms of German surrender to the effect that dismemberment could occur if the three controlling powers thought it necessary for future security. Although most comments about Russian foreign policy motives are sheer speculation, the strong Russian support for a commitment to dismemberment may well have stemmed from Soviet fears that a united Germany might eventually join in some sort of anti-Soviet bloc. Stalin had great contempt for the German character and had expressed grave doubts that the Germans had the courage or intelligence to become believing communists. Later Western speculation that Stalin had hoped to expand communism by moving into all of Germany is belied by the Russian's support for dismemberment, his consistent dismissal of the Germans as unready for such revolutionary changes, and his willingness to accept a specific zone of occupation at a time when Russian military forces appeared likely to conquer the largest portion of Germany. As Roosevelt pointed out at Yalta, the zones of occupation could well serve as the beginning of a permanent partition of Germany, and Stalin appeared to prefer a concrete accomplishment to grander schemes. That argument, as presented by the president, may have been suggested at some point by Stettinius or someone else from the State Department. The evidence is scanty, but on February 1, only a few days before the Yalta Conference began, Ambassador Winant in London claimed that current thinking was that zonal autonomy and control would increase substantially, thus effectively dividing Germany into three separate and compartmented zones (see Document 32). Although much of this came from British sources, it is probable that similar ideas had developed within the State Department. Given Roosevelt's earlier strong commitment to dismemberment, such an argument could explain his willingness to postpone the issue by referring the details of partitioning to a committee on the dismemberment of Germany.

The lengthy arguments over the role of France in any German settlement again stemmed from Anglo-Russian concern over the postwar power relationships in Europe. The Russians obviously feared the creation of some sort of Anglo-French entente against the Soviet Union, which was in fact the precise goal of British policy by that time. Nonetheless, Roosevelt's firm statement that American troops would not remain in Europe more than two years after victory apparently troubled Stalin. The British had never possessed sufficient military strength to restrain Germany in the west, and unless such restraint were possible the British might well begin thinking in terms of appeasing the Germans—again. Given that conundrum, Stalin appears to have concluded that taking a chance on Anglo-French cooperation was a better bet than relying on some sort of vague and ineffective controls against a resurgence of German power. In spite of Roosevelt's long-standing distrust of the French and particularly of deGaulle, the State Department argument that the United States should do all it could to restore France to her former status as a stable world power eventually won out. Moreover, since the president assumed a relatively brief American presence in Central Europe after the war, British appeals for assistance from France in policing Europe appeared more persuasive. By the close of the Yalta talks, Roosevelt had made the new American position clear, and Stalin—who rarely fought for lost causes—acquiesced.

For the first time in the war, reparations became the most crucial and troublesome issue regarding Germany. As Morgenthau had long feared, discussions of German reparations did not really consider the prevention of World War III. When the Soviet negotiators made their demands for immediate and extensive removals of industrial plants plus a ten-year reparations-in-kind program, Churchill attacked the proposals as unreasonable and impractical. Roosevelt, ever mindful of the post-World War I experience, worried aloud that American money might have to finance such long-term reparations as well as some program to prevent the Germans from starving. That, thought the president, was unacceptable. Roosevelt expressed great sympathy for the suffering and destruction endured by the Russians, and agreed they were entitled to extensive reparations, but his eventual suggestion that the question be referred to a special reparations committee smacks of typical Rooseveltian procrastination (see Document 33). The president's concern over avoiding any sort of American-financed relief program for the Germans, plus the general tendency of the Yalta talks toward increased Allied control over (and hence responsibility for) Germany, rang the death knell for the Morgenthau Plan, at least as an alternative under consideration by the president.

One aspect of Roosevelt's conduct at Yalta can be neither resolved nor ignored, and that is his health. Roosevelt suffered from congestive heart failure and had undergone treatment for heart disease since early in the war. Even his closest friends had commented in their private diaries about his physical deterioration by the fall of 1944. Although the president's personal physician, Admiral Ross McIntire, claimed that Roosevelt's mental processes had not been affected—a statement backed up by a heart specialist whom McIntire brought in on the case—other observers disagreed. Whatever the effect of the president's health at Yalta, the comment of Churchill's personal physician, Lord Moran, is worth noting:

> To a doctor's eye, the President appears a very sick man. He has all the symptoms or hardening of the arteries of the brain in an advanced stage, so that I give him only a few months to live. But men shut their eyes when they do not want to see, and the Americans here cannot bring themselves to believe that he is finished.[14]

Whether or not Roosevelt's physical condition played a significant part in his policies and tactics at Yalta, however, is another question. Historians have frequently commented that he did not have the strength to battle Stalin, but such direct confrontations were so alien to Roosevelt's style and personality that a hands-down struggle with the Russians was unlikely regardless of his energy level. On the German question, at any rate, Roosevelt followed a line of reasoning which was consistent with his previous policies. He kept the Russians relatively happy, he avoided fixed commitments wherever possible, and he avoided any long-term American entanglement in Europe. The effects of poor health became far more apparent after Yalta when Roosevelt, exhausted by the strain of the conference, was no longer able to play the game of balancing his executive departments against each other. With the president spending more time resting at Warm Springs, Georgia, normal bureaucratic patterns asserted themselves and the State Department, in consultation with the military, took over the direction of foreign policy.

For Germany, Yalta served only to mark time. No final decisions appeared, but the outlines of the final settlement had begun to develop. Occupation zones and boundary adjustments substituted for dismemberment; what the Russians called "a modest but decent standard of living" for the Germans replaced pastoralization; coordinated administration and control via a Central Control Commission eliminated the concept of making the Germans responsible for their own problems; and deindustrialization was limited to "industry that could be used for military production" (see Documents 34, 35). Only denazification seemed in the spirit of the Morgenthau Plan. Even limiting reparations to compensation in kind covered over the general agreement that the Soviet Union deserved a level of reparations which might force the rehabilitation of German industry. But Yalta was a meeting of politicians and diplomats, not bureaucrats and mid-rank Army officers assigned the job of administering occupied Germany. Unaware of the nuances and particulars of the Yalta decisions, such people simply continued to plan on the basis of previous policy guidelines—the old "Army Handbook" and JCS 1067.

Notes

1. Minutes to the Foreign Office on Halifax, September 14, 1944, No. 4941, FO 371/39080/4010, paper C12073/146/G18, Public Record Office, London, England.

2. Handwritten note on draft of "Germany is Our Problem," November 16, 1944 and February 12, 1945, Harry Dexter White Papers, Princeton University Library, Princeton, N.J.

3. The British Chiefs of Staff were the top military organization in that country, similar to the American Joint Chiefs of Staff.

4. U.S., Department of State, *Foreign Relations of the United States: Conference at Quebec, 1944*, Memo by White of Conversation of September 13, 1944 (Washington, D.C.: Government Printing Office, 1972), p. 326.

5. Henry L. Stimson and McGeorge Bundy, *On Active Service in Peace and War* (New York: Harper & Brothers, 1948), p. 581.

6. Minutes to the Foreign Office on "Political Situation in the United States: Weekly Political Summary," October 11, 1944, FO 371/38548/4206, paper AN 3859/261, Public Record Office, London.

7. The Joint Chiefs of Staff consisted of the military commanders of the United States Army and Navy, and other officers appointed by the president.

8. See Document 28. Actor Richard Burton, in an article written shortly after he had played Winston Churchill in an adaptation of a portion of Churchill's memoirs, claimed that performing the role had been a depressing experience, because of the prime minister's bloodthirsty vindictiveness. Burton received a thorough scolding from various Churchill defenders. Nevertheless, unless one chooses to dismiss Churchill's statements to Stalin as mere rhetoric, a reading of the minutes of the TOLSTOY Conference lends some credence to the finding of Burton's artistic sensitivity. Not surprisingly, Churchill makes no mention in his memoirs of his strong support for a harsh and punitive German settlement. The Burton article, "To Play Churchill Is to Hate Him," is in the *New York Times*, section 2, November 24, 1974. Some of the responses can be found in the *New York Times* issue of December 8, 1974. Another small but revealing entry in this potentially endless debate is Churchill's response to a suggestion in February, 1945, that British policy should be to help the Italians as much as possible since that was why they had fought the war—"to secure liberty and a decent existence for the peoples of Europe." Churchill responded, "Not a bit of it: we are fighting to secure the proper respect for the British people!" *The Diaries of Sir Alexander Cadogan, 1938-1945*, ed. David Dilks (New York: G.P. Putnam's Sons, 1972), p. 711.

9. De Gaulle was recognized shortly before this time by Roosevelt and Churchill as the leader of the provisional government in liberated France.

10. Smuts to Churchill, October 29, 1944, PREM 3/192/3/53, Public Record Office, London.

11. Churchill to Smuts, October 30, 1944, PREM 3/192/3/52, Public Record Office, London.

12. Roosevelt to Churchill, November 13, 1944, Map Rool Collection, No. 647, Franklin D. Roosevelt Papers, Franklin D. Roosevelt Library, Hyde Park, N.Y.

13. Although the bitter and tendentious arguments over the entire question of the boundaries and government of postwar Poland are largely tangential to the German problem, some brief mention of Anglo-American policy is in order. There is still a real need for a thoughtful, comprehensive, and nonideological essay on the Policy issue in Anglo-American-Soviet relations between 1941 and 1956. My comment about the attitude held by State Department and Foreign Office officials comes from reading repeated references to the dominant Soviet position in Poland or comments which indicated that Britain and America needed a Polish settlement which looked (rather than was) good. That, of course, is in conflict with many of the arguments set forth during Anglo-American negotiations with the Russians. Three elements seem to make up the Polish issue: appearances, a true desire to see a Poland which was not a Soviet client-state, and a belief that the line had to be drawn somewhere with the Russians, so why not in Poland—even if victory seemed unlikely. It is worth noting that Churchill was under heavy attack in early 1945 for his harsh suppression of the anti-Monarchists in Greece.

14. Lord Moran, *Churchill: Taken from the Diaries of Lord Moran*, (Boston: Houghton Mifflin Co., 1966), p. 242. Moran's comment may at least partially be a result of the power of suggestion, since he had received only a few days before a letter from an American physician, who wrote that Roosevelt had had heart trouble eight months earlier and was obviously very ill. *Ibid*, pp. 242-43. Moran was not a practiced diagnostician, nor do trained observers agree on the meaning of Roosevelt's symptoms. Nevertheless, the question of Roosevelt's health raises troubling issues regarding the transfer of authority in the event of serious illness.

5

Death as Decision-Maker: The Rejection of the Morgenthau Plan

During the few months between the Yalta Conference and the death of Roosevelt, United States policy toward Germany received little guidance from the top. Hopkins told Eden in April, 1945, that Roosevelt had not initialed most of the thirty-seven cables sent over the presidential signature to Churchill since the Crimea meeting. Although none of those messages concerned postwar Germany, Hopkins's remark indicates that Roosevelt no longer directed American foreign policy with any consistency.

Even so, presidential approbation remained important and the State, Treasury, and War departments made attempts to obtain presidential sanction for their programs, but to no avail. Roosevelt refused to commit himself fully one way or the other. After approving a State Department memo which called for a centralized administration rather than control by the military governors of each zone, Roosevelt backed off when Stimson and Morgenthau protested—Stimson because army policy was to maintain complete freedom of action, and Morgenthau because control implied responsibility and the possibility of reconstructing the German economy.[1] Eventually, on March 23, the president approved a policy statement drafted by the War Department (*Alternative 2:* see Document 36). That directive, Roosevelt's last on the German question, demonstrates how far American policy had moved since the Quebec memorandum and the concept of pastoralization. Fighting a holding action, Morgenthau and his advisors had to accept the War Department's suggestion that some basic industries, including coal production, be retained in order to meet the needs of the occupying forces and to prevent disease, starvation, or civil unrest. Roosevelt's natural penchant for avoiding decisions made the War Department position of postponing any consideration of long-term economic matters appealing. Moreover, McCloy told Morgenthau that the president had flatly endorsed the moderate War Department approach since he wanted to change the character of German industry, not destroy it. The Germans would have to support themselves, although without reentering the world export market. In almost every other plan which came from sources other than the Treasury Department, a reference to eliminating Germany's war-making industries appeared; but by 1945 such references had become as *pro forma* as spinning a prayer wheel, and they failed to explain how to limit industry to only peaceful forms. The Morgenthau Plan had its last shot at success in the March, 1945, War Department proposal. In spite of some ambiguity and obliqueness, the economic sections reflected Treasury Department thinking in calling for very limited production capabilities, no extensions of credit to Germany except with special permission of the Control Council, and economic decentralization with basic responsibility for the economy resting with German authorities.

Not surprisingly, bureaucratic warfare broke out anew. The State, Treasury, and War departments, and a new entrant—the Foreign Economic Administration—struggled to establish their views on postwar Germany, using as a vehicle the revision of JCS 1067. That revision, approved by president Harry S. Truman on May 11, 1945, remained official American occupation policy until July, 1947. That, however, is a misleading statement. The War Department's desire for flexibility with directives which left specifics up to the military occupation authorities eventually became the Trojan horse which Morgenthau had predicted. Although arguments in favor of military autonomy reflected fears of internal rebellion and chaos, when conflicts with the French and the Russians arose, JCS 1067 did not limit the response of occupation officials.

The real impact of the War Department attitude was hinted at when, early in April, Secretary Stimson, concerned about the postwar economic development of Germany, raised the question of instructing General Eisenhower to bypass the Ruhr industrial region in his military operations. Although the military leaders in Washington indicated reluctance to interfere with a field commander's complete freedom of action in military operations, General Marshall did make an informal inquiry about Eisenhower's intentions (see Document 37). Ever sensitive to political factors, Eisenhower quickly responded that, even though he had to eliminate all German military forces in the Ruhr, he hoped to avoid unnecessary destruction of industrial facilities. So much for Treasury hopes that the war itself would achieve a major step towards deindustrialization.

The Morgenthau Plan and the Cold War

At three forty-five in the afternoon of April 12, 1945, President Franklin D. Roosevelt died—and the Morgenthau Plan for Germany died with him. Roosevelt and Morgenthau had always agreed upon one central fact regarding the people, not merely their Nazi leaders. Roosevelt never ceased to condemn "German" crimes, and whenever State and War department spokesmen moved the president toward a separation of Nazi and German guilt, Morgenthau could always pull him back with an appeal to Roosevelt's intense dislike and distrust of the overall German character; a character which the president believed had been Prussianized.

Some, particularly those who favored the complete rehabilitation of Germany from the start, argued that the spirit and substance of the Morgenthau Plan for Germany lived on in JCS 1067 and the actions of the occupation authorities until at least 1946 and the decision of the American high commissioner in Germany, General Lucius D. Clay. to halt reparations payments to the Soviet Union. But that distorts the nature and purpose of the Morgenthau Plan. Morgenthau's proposals included harsh punishment, particularly in the form of a refusal by the Allies to accept any responsibility for the economic well-being of the German population, but the goal of the plan never centered on revenge. From the beginning the ultimate aim of the program was the complete and effective reform of German national character and society.

Some have claimed that the Potsdam agreements of August, 1945, between the American, British, and Russian governments, modified but did not really change the thrust of the Morgenthau Plan. That is far from the case. The Potsdam Conference, attended by Stalin, the new American president Truman, and the two British prime ministers—Churchill and his successor Clement Atlee—dealt extensively with the problem of Germany. Truman, who later claimed in his memoirs that he had opposed the Morgenthau Plan from the outset, has a well-deserved reputation for decisiveness, but he also tended to follow the advice of the military and State Department Professionals. Although the new president temporarily favored dismemberment of Germany, his secretary of state, James F. Byrnes, convinced Truman not to present such a program at the Potsdam talks.

But to discuss piecemeal the various portions of the Morgenthau Plan which seemed to crop up after April, 1945, is to warp the nature of Morgenthau's proposal. Unless the Morgenthau Plan existed as a whole, it did not exist at all. Revenge, disarmament, dismemberment, punishment, and programs of democratization could and did exist without being part of that overall plan; but their goals were not the same as those offered by Morgenthau and the Treasury Department. With the death of Roosevelt, Morgenthau quickly lost his privileged position in the American government. On July 14, 1945, President Truman accepted the Treasury Secretary's prearranged resignation, and the Morgenthau Plan for Germany was left without a sponsor.

Truman's statement in his memoirs that he had always opposed the concept of the Morgenthau Plan may well be a piece of after-the-fact Cold War rhetoric, for when he wrote those memoirs, Truman was most eager to demonstrate his record as a staunch anticommunist. But the attitude of the American high commissioner in Germany from 1945 through 1949, General Clay, as expressed in messages written early in the first few months after V-E Day (Victory in Europe) indicate the direction of his thinking. Policy for Germany had to be shifted from concern for preventing rearmament to concern for preventing economic collapse, and those persons who still thought in terms of the Morgenthau Plan had a warped sense of judgment (*Alternative 2:* see Documents 38, 39, and 40). Clay's attitude is critical to an understanding of policy for, as John McCloy later recalled, the American military governor did exactly what the War Department expected; he utilized the escape clauses in JCS 1067 and made the directive fit army policy without the chore of pushing another revision through the bureaucracy. The desire to punish the Germans, supposedly a residue of the Morgenthau Plan, clearly conflicted with Clay's concept of the two choices which existed for Germany—communism or democracy (see Document 40).

And where does that leave the Morgenthau Plan in the scheme of history? After all is said and done, does it really matter that the plan even existed if it died so premature a death? If what actually happened is the only concern of historians, then the answer is obvious. But alternatives, even if rejected, are a part of history; they offer penetrating insights into the minds and motives of decision-makers.

Two small but persistent myths about the Morgenthau Plan need to be firmly dismissed. The first is the idea that Roosevelt did not really understand the meaning of the Morgenthau Plan when he initialed the joint memorandum with Churchill during the Quebec Conference. In spite of his deteriorating health, there can be no doubt that the president understood and agreed with the Treasury Department proposal. His earlier concern for an overall reform of the German character, often expressed in seemingly antic comments against goose-stepping and uniforms, followed by his vigorous support for an improved foreign trade situation in postwar Britain, indicate his awareness of the nature of Morgenthau's proposal. That it fit into his overall (if ill-defined) concept of Soviet-American cooperation—since the Russians apparently supported the plan—only added to the proposal's attractiveness.

The second is the claim that the Morgenthau Plan gave Nazi propagandists a field day and was "worth thirty divisions to the Germans."[2] Hull made such arguments to the president shortly after the Quebec Conference, and General Marshall did tell Morgenthau that German resistance had stiffened shortly after the American press broke the story of the Morgenthau Plan. On the other hand, Nazi Propaganda Minister Joseph Goebbels had long claimed that the destruction of the German nation would follow any German defeat. The Morgenthau Plan may have added some credibility to such appeals to German nationalism, but it hardly initiated that propaganda. More effective German defense in the late fall of 1944 came from military, not psychological, actions. Their victory at Arnhem, which prevented a quick charge into Germany by Anglo-American forces, occurred just as the Morgenthau Plan story hit the newspapers, and probably did far more for the morale of the German troops than any fears of what postwar plans the Allies had in store for them.

To take the question of American policy toward postwar Germany beyond Roosevelt is to enter into an essentially new and different set of policy alternatives worthy of a separate study. With the inauguration of Truman as president, a new approach to foreign policy began. Moreover, Truman faced a different set of problems. Whether Soviet-American confrontation—the Cold War—came to dominate America's policy toward Germany in 1945 or in 1946, or even later, is essentially moot, for there can be no denying that the specter of Russian power and communist expansion rearmed and integrated Germany into the Western alliance. Some have argued that French opposition to four-power cooperation in Germany during a crucial period from the end of the war until early 1946 ruined the one great opportunity to take advantage of Russian desires to develop a quadripartite administration of Germany. However, that line of reasoning seemingly ignores the broader scope of Soviet-American relations. Mutual distrust is frequently a self-fulfilling prophecy, and such distrust had certainly existed between the two nations since the Russian Revolution in 1917. French vetoes in the Allied Control Council may have blocked early steps toward Soviet—American cooperation in Germany, but the confrontations in Turkey, Iran, Greece, and Russian occupied Eastern Europe did not occur because the French feared any sort of unified Germany. Moreover, both the United States and the Soviet Union could count on French opposition to any real movement toward an effective joint administration of Germany, which left them free to posture and still leave all their options open.

In fact, it is easier to argue that the policies of Franklin Roosevelt toward the Soviet Union, even with all their ambiguities and hedging, were an aberration rather than the norm. Antagonism toward Soviet Russia had been a hallmark of American policy until Roosevelt extended diplomatic recognition in 1933, and that antagonism soon came to characterize the Truman administration within a few months after Roosevelt's death. Truman was eager to resolve the Soviet-American confrontation but only on American terms; that is, through containment. Since the containment concept had as a premise the belief that communism contained within itself a set of irresolvable tensions (i.e., the seeds of its own destruction), patience and firmness became the tools of victory, not accommodation. Such a desire for foreign policy success is hardly reprehensible (after all, the president swears an oath to achieve such nationalistic goals), but we should not pretend that the United States followed a policy of conciliation, accommodation,and cooperation in an attempt to create a situation where two very different political/economic systems could coexist and work with each other. Truman's instinctive reaction to Soviet policies was suspicion and belligerence, and his occasional statements about carrying on Roosevelt's policy of cooperation become meaningless in the absence of real action.

Any discussion of the Morgenthau Plan for Germany cannot avoid some speculation on the structure of Europe and elsewhere had it been implemented. Certainly it would have meant much more than just a world without the Volkswagen. The one alternative which Truman really never considered was the strong and insistent pursuit of a neutralized and decentralized Germany. That alone would have reshaped and changed the basic structure of the Cold War. Possibly it would have helped to create a change for the worse, if we assume that Soviet belligerence toward the West existed without regard for Western policies; possibly for the better, if we assume that Russian fears of Germany were historic and real and that Soviet policies reflected, at least in part, the actions of the Western nations. Even if tension and conflict between powerful nation-states is inevitable, the intensity of the Cold War has proceeded from specific issues. Germany, where Soviet and American power physically met, was the greatest issue of all. The Morgenthau Plan did not have improved Soviet-American relations as a primary goal, but a weak and neutral Germany lay at the very heart of the proposal. When the American government finally threw out the Morgenthau Plan for Germany, it threw out the baby with the bath water; for not only did the United States eschew a policy of revenge, but it also tossed away programs which could have established a truly neutral, disengaged Germany. That alternative might have, with relatively little risk, significantly diminished the tension and length of the Cold War.

Notes

1. Roosevelt claimed to have absolutely no recollection of having signed the State Department memo. Whether that was a result of his health or his dissembling cannot be determined—though Morgenthau attributed it to illness.

2. Statement by Lt. Col. John Boettiger, as quoted in John Wheeler-Bennett and Anthony Nichols, *The Semblance of Peace* (London: Macmillan & Co., 1972), p. 185n. Boettiger was a son-in-law of President Roosevelt.

Part two

Documents of the Decision

1

The Quebec Memorandum

This memorandum apparently committed Roosevelt and Churchill to an extreme form of the Morgenthau Plan. Brief but unambiguous, it went against the bulk of opinion in both the British and American governments. Roosevelt soon began to hedge on his commitment, and Churchill quickly followed suit. Nonetheless, the shock waves created by this memorandum stimulated responses in the American bureaucracy which resulted in some portions of the harsh peace approach being permanently written into occupation directives. This memorandum is evidence that Roosevelt had considered Soviet cooperation in the postwar world as probable. It completely eliminated any chance of Germany becoming a factor in the postwar power equation.

Document†

At a conference between the President and the Prime Minister upon the best measures to prevent renewed rearmament by Germany, it was felt that an essential feature was the future disposition of the Ruhr and the Saar.

The ease with which the metallurgical, chemical and electric industries in Germany can be converted from peace to war has already been impressed upon us by bitter experience. It must also be remembered that the Germans have devastated a large portion of the industries of Russia and of other neighbouring Allies, and it is only in accordance with justice that these injured countries should be entitled to losses they have suffered. The industries referred to in the Ruhr and in the Saar would therefore be necessarily put out of action and closed down. It was felt that the two districts should be put under some body under the world organization which would supervise the dismantling of these industries and make sure that they were not started up again by some subterfuge.

This programme for eliminating the war-making industries in the Ruhr and in the Saar is looking forward to converting Germany into a country primarily agricultural and pastoral in its character.

The Prime Minister and the President were in agreement upon this programme.

(Intd.) O.K.

F.D.R.

(Intd.)W.S.C.

15 9.

†From: Memorandum Initialed by Roosevelt and Churchill, September 15, 1944, in U.S., Department of State, *Foreign Relations of the United States (FRUS), Conference at Quebec, 1944* (Washington, D.C. Government Printing Office, 1972) pp. 466-67.

2

================ A Meeting of the Minds

During discussions with Eden in March, 1943, Roosevelt clearly expressed his support for the dismemberment of Germany and his belief that the Soviet Union also supported that policy. The president's distrust of the situation in postwar France is evident from his hope that German disarmament would make French rearmament unnecessary. Eden's belief that Stalin had no desire to be saddled with a defeated Germany contrasts strikingly with the Cold War assumption that the Soviet Union had always planned to conquer as much of Europe as it could.

Document†

...*Germany*. Eden said that the most important thing we had to get a meeting of the minds on in regard to Germany was the question of whether we were going to be able to deal with Germany as a unit after the war, disarming them, etc., and also for the peace, or whether we were going to insist that it be broken up into several independent states. Eden said that from the conferences he had had with the Russians he was sure that Stalin would not trust the Germans; that in his speech the other day when he said the Russian armies were going to stop at the German Border, this was for propaganda purposes inside Germany (Eden believed); that he, Stalin, has a deepseated distrust of the Germans and that he will insist that Germany be broken up into a number of states. The President said he hoped we would not use the methods discussed at Versailles and also promoted by Clemenceau to arbitrarily divide Germany, but thought that we should encourage the differences and ambitions that will spring up within Germany for a Separatist Movement and, in effect, approve of a division which represents German public opinion.

I asked what they would do if that spontaneous desire did not spring up and both the President and Eden agreed that, under any circumstances, Germany must be divided into several states, one of which must, over all circumstances, by Prussia. The Prussians cannot be permitted to dominate all Germany.

Eden said he believed that one of the reasons Stalin wanted a second front in Europe was political; that if Germany collapsed he had no desire, in Germany, to take the full responsibility for what would happen in Germany or the rest of Europe, and he believed it was a fixed matter of Russian foreign

†From: Memorandum by Hopkins of Conversation with Eden and Roosevelt, March 15, 1943, in U.S., Department of State, *FRUS, 1943* (Washington, D.C.: Government Printing Office, 1963), vol. 3, pp. 16–17.

policy to have both British and United States troops heavily in Europe when the collapse comes. Eden expressed this purely as his private opinion and said that he was sure that in Russia a different view was held in some quarters but, nevertheless, he thought he had stated Stalin's position.

We, then, discussed, at some length, the political effect of our troops being in Italy as against France at the time of the collapse of Germany and, while both Eden and the President thought it would not be as advantageous it was far better than not being there at all.

I told the President it was important that we have the frankest kind of talk with Mr. Eden about potential differences in Europe and that, at the moment, I saw two—1, The people of Serbia and Croatia and, 2, the problem of what countries, free and otherwise, should be disarmed in Europe. I felt that from what Mr. Eden had said he would not believe in a disarmed Poland or France and I thought it would be very unfortunate if he went back to London without fully understanding the President's position in this, even if he did not fully agree and that he, Eden, should tell the Presdient, frankly, what his objections [were] to the disarmament of countries like France and Poland. The President reiterated to Eden what he had told Churchill, that after Germany is disarmed what is the reason for France having a big military establishment?

3

The State Department on Germany, September, 1943

In preparation for Secretary of State Hull's trip to Moscow in October, 1943, the State Department's *ad hoc* Interdivisional Country Committee on Germany prepared a strong recommendation against partition and in favor of the political reintegration of Germany. Arguing that a democratic government could survive in Germany only under favorable conditions, the committee recommended in strong terms that the German economy be rehabilitated. The tone of the document clearly indicates the strong feelings of distrust and antagonism toward the Soviet Union which were held by many State Department officials. Without saying so, the report recommends that Germany join some sort of Western entente against the spread of communism.

Document†

The Political Reorganization of Germany

I. PARTITION

The Departmental Committee on Germany unanimously recommends that the United States Government oppose the enforced break-up of Germany as a part of the peace settlement.

The Committee bases its recommendation on the following considerations:

1. The crucial means of attaining security against further German aggression for some time to come will be controls to insure military and economic disarmament. If these controls are effectively enforced Germany will be incapable of waging war.

2. These measures will have to be maintained whether Germany is partitioned or left intact. Partition would make no useful contribution either to occupation or to the administration of the basic controls; it might, on the contrary, complicate the administration and, by setting up separate zones, lead to friction between the victor powers over the character of the occupation and the treatment of the several regions.

†From: "The Political Reorganization of Germany," Recommendation of the Inter-divisional Country Committee, September 23, 1943, in *Postwar Foreign Policy Preparation, 1939-1945,* by Harley A. Notter, Department of the State Publication 3580 (Washington, D.C.: Government Printing Office, 1949), pp. 558-59.

3. Because of the high degree of economic, political and cultural integration in Germany it is to be anticipated that partition would have to be imposed and maintained by external force and that such action would evoke a greatly increased resentment on the part of the German people to the serious detriment of their ultimate recondiliation with the peace settlement.

4. An imposed partition would require the enforcement of sweeping measures, over and above the basic military and economic controls, to prevent surreptitious collaboration of the partite states and to restrain the nationalistic drive for reunification. The victor powers would consequently impose on themselves through partition a burden unnecessary for the attainment of security and would give to the Germans, equally without necessity, a ready-made program of national resurgence at the expense of the peace.

5. By the tests of effectiveness, enforceability and continued acceptability to both victors and vanquished, partition would make no contribution to security and would, on the contrary, create such bitterness and require such rigorous methods of enforcement that it would constitute a grave danger to future world order.

II. DEMOCRACY

The Departmental Committee on Germany believes that it would be unwise for the United Nations to disinterest themselves in the kind of government which will be established in Germany after the war. The potentialities for evil on the part of a reviewed aggressive state point to the desirability of every feasible effort to prevent the resurgence of a government and people dominated by excessive nationalism. The committee anticipates that there will be strong incentives for individual states to exercise influence and suggests that the best means of forestalling such a dangerous procedure would be an agreement among the principal United Nations for a common policy insofar as it can be achieved.

The committee is of opinion that, in the long run, the most desirable form of government for Germany would be a broadly-based democracy operating under a bill of rights to protect the civil and political liberties of the individual.

The committee is under no illusions as to the difficulties in the way of creating an effective democracy in Germany. It suggests that there are three conditions under which a new democratic experiment might survive:

1. A tolerable standard of living.

2. A minimum of bitterness against the peace terms in order, insofar as possible, to avoid an appealing program for future nationalistic upheavals at home and disturbances abroad. The committee is aware that the occupation and the permanent security controls which it deems imperative will give offense to many Germans, but it recommends, because of the importance of ultimate German reconciliation with the peace settlement, that the measures be kept to the minimum in number and in severity which will be compatible with security.

3. A harmony of policy between the British and American Governments on the one hand and the Soviet Government on the other. In case of friction Germany would be in a position to hold the balance of power with disastrous results both for treaty limitations and for political stability at home. The Soviet Government, in turn, would be in a position to use the Communist strength in Germany to the great disadvantage of the internal political peace of Germany and to the comparably great advantage of Russian interests.

The committee therefore recommends that the United States Government adopt, in the interest of fostering moderate government in Germany, the principle of a program looking to the economic recovery of Germany, to the earliest possible reconciliation of the German people with the peace, and to the assimilation of Germany, as soon as would be compatible with security considerations, into the projected international order. The Committee further recommends that the Soviet Government be invited to give its support to a new democratic experiment and to the principle of the suggested program.

The committee believes that there is a marked disadvantage, both from the viewpoint of political warfare against National Socialism and from the viewpoint of preparing the democratic forces of Germany for action, in the failure of the United States and British Governments to announce their support of future German democracy. The committee likewise believes that the recent appearance of a democratic German program under tacit Russian patronage might serve to give the Communists control of the democratic movement, and therefore establish a Russian hegemony in Germany, unless Anglo-American support encourages the moderates to participate and make the movement genuinely democratic. . . .

4

Roosevelt on Germany: October, 1943

During conversations just preceding Hull's trip to Moscow, State Department officials learned of the president's strong support for a political but no economic dismemberment of Germany. With the historically exaggerated success of the *Zollverein* (a customs union among the German states that existed prior to the unification of Germany under Prussia) clearly in mind, Roosevelt dismissed arguments that such Germany-wide economic cooperation would not work without concomitant political unity. As of those conversations on October 5, 1943, the president obviously had no plan to deindustrialize Germany beyond the elimination of all arms-making capabilities. Later in the same meeting, Roosevelt admitted that his reliance on memories of a trip to Germany taken twenty-five years earlier might be misplaced.

Document†

Germany

The President stated categorically that he favors partition of Germany into three or more states, completely sovereign but joined by a network of common services as regards postal arrangements, communications, railways, customs, perhaps power (although he thought power arrangements should be made on a continental basis), etc. The new German states should be deprived of all military activities, including training, and of armament industries. East Prussia should be detached, and all dangerous elements of the population forcibly removed. As against the argument that partition would have many undesirable results and that the customs union arrangement would either prove to be unworkable or become a powerful instrument of re-unification, the President stated that we are inclined to exaggerate these effects. Later in the discussion, however, the President said that the whole transitional period would have to be one of trial and error, and that it may well happen that in practice we shall discover that partition, undertaken immediately after the war, may have to be abandoned. As regards reparation, there will be no exaction in money, but rather in manpower and equipment....

†From: Memorandum of Conversation with Roosevelt and State Department Officials, in U.S., Department of State, *FRUS, 1943*, vol. 1, p. 542.

5

Roosevelt and the Joint Chiefs of Staff, November, 1943

Aboard the USS *Iowa*, enroute to the Cairo meetings with Churchill and the Teheran Conference with Churchill and Stalin in November and December, 1943, Roosevelt met with his Joint Chiefs of Staff. Although the primary topic of conversation related to military strategy, the possibility of an early and complete German surrender or collapse (*RANKIN*) necessitated a consideration of American policy for postwar occupation. Two themes predominate: the president's desire for the partitioning of Germany, and his absolute refusal to become involved in the problems of postwar France. The president's policies clearly presume a harmonious relationship with the Soviet Union.

Document†

Spheres of Responsibility in Germany— Europe-Wide "Rankin"

The President observed that in the memorandum he received from Admiral Leahy on behalf of the Joint Chiefs of Staff asking for guidance regarding spheres of influence as a result of a European-wide Rankin, the paper makes certain suppositions without actually saying so. He felt that whatever territorial dispositions were made should conform to geographic subdivisions of Germany. He said that the Soviet Government will offer no objection to breaking up Germany after the war, that practically speaking there should be three German states after the war, possibly five. He said (1) we might take southern Germany, Baden, Wurtenburg [*Württemberg*], Bavaria, everything south of the Rhine [*Main?*]. This area forms a sort of southern state. (2) Take everything north and west of that area, including Hamburg and Hanover, and so forth, up to and including Berlin to form a second state, and the northeastern part, that is, Prussia, Pomerania, and south, to form a third state. He believed these general divisions were a logical basis for splitting up

†From: Minutes of the President's Meeting with the Joint Chiefs of Staff, November 19, 1943, in U.S., Department of State,*FRUS, Conference at Cairo and Teheran, 1943* (Washington, D.C.: Government Printing Office, 1961), pp. 253-54, 255-56.

Germany. Especially was this so because the first or southern state was largely Roman Catholic; the northwestern portion is Protestant, while it might be said that the religion of the northeastern part is Prussianism. He felt that Marshal Stalin might "okay" such a division. He believed that the Chiefs of Staff would want to make a European Rankin conform to such a division. Actually the British wanted the northwestern part of Germany and would like to see the U.S. take France and Germany south of the Moselle River. He said he did not like that arrangement. We do not want to be concerned with reconstituting France. France is a British "baby." United States is not popular in France at the present time. The British should have France, Luxembourg, Belgium, Baden, Bavaria, and Wurtenburg. The occupation of these places should be British. The United States should take northwest Germany. We can get our ships into such ports as Bremen and Hamburg, also Norway and Denmark, and we should go as far as Berlin. The Soviets could then take the territory to the east thereof. The United States should have Berlin. The British plan for the United States to have southern Germany, and he (the President) did not like. . . .

The President said he felt that the divisions now in North Africa, Sicily and Italy should be the divisions first to be sent back to the United States. He said one reason for the political "headache" in France was that De Gaulle hoped to be one mile behind the troops in taking over the government. He felt that we should get out of France and Italy as soon as possible, letting the British and the French handle their own problem together. There would definitely be a race for Berlin. We may have to put the United States divisions into Berlin as soon as possible.

Admiral Leahy observed it would be easy to go directly into northwest Germany. The problem of occupational troops proceeding to northwest Germany would certainly be less difficult than their fighting their way there across the intervening territory from northwestern France.

General Marshall observed that it was most important to keep commands in homogeneous control.

The President said he envisaged a railroad invasion of Germany with little or no fighting.

General Marshall said he assumed there would be a difficult lack of rolling stock and the land advance would have to be largely made on a motor truck basis.

Mr. Hopkins suggested that we be ready to put an airborne division into Berlin two hours after the collapse of Germany.

In reply to a question from the President as to Admiral Leahy's opinion of the occupational area divisions, from a State Department point of view, Admiral Leahy said that he felt we should definitely get out of France as soon as possible. We should accept any difficulties in order to get out of France at the earliest possible time. If we want to let De Gaulle have France, all well and good. However, whatever troops there are in France at the time of German collapse will certainly have to stay in order to supervise any elections. General De Gaulle wants to start the French Government right now. Possibly there will be civil war in France. The British should clear up such a condition. On the other hand, it would be much easier for the United States to handle conditions in Germany. The Germans are easier to handle than would be the French under the chaotic conditions that could be expected in France.

The President said he personally envisaged an occupational force of about one million United States troops. He expanded on the policy of "quarantine." He said that the four United Nations by their police power could, if necessary, maintain order in Europe by the "quarantine" method. For instance, we do not want to use our troops in settling local squabbles in such a place as Yugoslavia. We could use the Army and Navy as an economic blockade and preclude ingress or egress to any area where disorder prevailed.

In reply to a question from General Marshall as to how long the President contemplated it would be necessary to maintain one million men in Europe, the President replied for at least one year, maybe two. . . .

6

The Teheran Conference

Although the Big Three made no binding commitment at Teheran to any specific formula for the dismemberment of Germany, they did agree on the principle of a partitioning of Germany after the war. Working in tandem against a slightly reluctant Winston Churchill, Stalin and Roosevelt also raised the issue of deindustrialization and seemed quite taken with the idea. Reparations, the issue which later caused a shift in Soviet policy regarding Germany's postwar economy, did not make an appearance during the Teheran discussions.

Document†

Turning to the question of Germany, The President said that the question was whether or not to split up Germany.

Marshal Stalin replied that they preferred the dismemberment of Germany.

The Prime Minister said he was all for it but that he was primarily more interested in seeing Prussia, the evil core of German militarism, separated from the rest of Germany.

The President said he had a plan that he had thought up some months ago for the division of Germany in five parts. These five parts were:

1. All Prussia to be rendered as small and weak as possible.
2. Hanover and Northwest section.
3. Saxony and Leipzig area.
4. Hesse—Darmstadt
   Hesse-Kassel and the area South of the Rhine.
5. Bavaria, Baden, and Wurtemburg [*Württemberg*].

He proposed that these five areas should be self-governed and that there should be two regions under United Nations or some form of International control. These were:

1. The area of the Kiel Canal and the City of Hamburg.
2. The Ruhr and the Saar, the latter to be used for the benefit of all Europe.

The Prime Minister said, to use an American expression, "The President had said a mouthful."

He went on to say that in his mind there were two considerations, one destructive and the other constructive.

1. The separation of Prussia from the rest of the Reich.

†From: Minutes of Tripartite Political Meeting, December 1, 1943, U.S., Department of State, *FRUS, Teheran*, pp. 600, 602-604.

2. To detach Bavaria, Baden, Wurtemburg [*Württemberg*] and the Palatinate from the rest of Germany and make them part of the Confederation of the Danube.

Marshal Stalin said he felt if Germany was to be dismembered, it should really be dismembered, and it was neither a question of the division of Germany in five or six states and two areas as the President suggested. However, he said he preferred the President's plan to the suggestion of Mr. Churchill.

He felt that to include German areas within the framework of large confederations would merely offer an opportunity to the German elements to revive a great State.

He went on to say that he did not believe there was a difference among Germans; that all German soldiers fought like devils and the only exception was the Austrians.

He said that the Prussian Officers and Staffs should be eliminated, but as to the inhabitants, he saw little difference between one part of Germany and another.

He said he was against the idea of confederation as artificial and one that would not last in that area, and in addition would provide opportunity for the German elements to control.

Austria, for example, had existed as an independent state and should again. Hungary, Rumania, and Bulgaria likewise.

The President said he agreed with the Marshal, particularly in regard to the absence of differences between Germans. He said fifty years ago there had been a difference but since the last war it was no longer so.

He said the only difference was that in Bavaria and the Southern part of Germany there was no officer cast[e] as there had been in Prussia. He agreed with Marshal Stalin that the Austrians were an exception.

The Prime Minister said he did not wish to be considered as against the dismemberment of Germany—quite the contrary, but he felt to separate the parts above would merely mean that sooner or later they will reunite into one nation and that the main thing was to keep Germany divided if only for fifty years.

Marshall Stalin repeated what he had said as to the danger of the re-unification of Germany. He said no matter what measures were adopted there would always be a strong urge on the part of the Germans to unite.

He said it was a great mistake to unite Hungary with Germans since the Germans would merely control the Hungarians and to create large frameworks within which the Germans could operate would be very dangerous.

He felt the whole purpose of any international organization to preserve peace would be to neutralize this tendency on the part of the Germans and apply against them economic and other measures and if necessary, force, to prevent their unification and revival. He said the victorious nations must have the strength to beat the Germans if they ever start on the path of a new war.

The Prime Minister inquired whether Marshal Stalin contemplated a Europe composed of little states, disjoined, separated and weak.

Marshal Stalin replied not Europe but Germany.

He supposed for example that Poland would be a strong country, and France, and Italy likewise; that Rumania and Bulgaria would remain as they always had; small States.

The President remarked Germany had been less dangerous to civilization when in 107 provinces.

The Prime Minister said he hoped for larger units.

The Prime Minister then returned to the question of Poland and said he was not asking for any agreement nor was he set on the matter but he had a statement which he would like to have the Marshal examine.

This statement suggested that Poland should obtain equal compensation in the West, including Eastern Prussia and frontiers on the Oder to compensate for the areas which would be in the Soviet Union.

The President interjected to say that one question in regard to Germany remained to be settled and that was what body should be empowered to study carefully the question of dismemberment of Germany.

It was agreed that the European Advisory Committee [*Commission*] would undertake this task.

7

Roosevelt on France and Germany, February, 1944

In this letter to Churchill, Roosevelt's main concern is the broad question of autonomy for SCAEF (Supreme Commander Allied Expeditionary Forces) in liberated France or occupied Germany. His approach to that problem is indicative of his overall approach to foreign policy decisions. Given the slightest excuse or rationale, he postponed any sort of binding, final decisions and let events decide the hard issues. The final paragraph of the letter demonstrates the depth of Roosevelt's desire to avoid entanglement in European politics, particularly anything to do with France.

Document†
President Roosevelt to the British Prime Minister (Churchill)

Washington, February 29, 1944

Dear Winston:—I have been worrying a good deal of late on account of the tendency of all of us to prepare for future events in such detail that we may be letting ourselves in for trouble when the time arrives.

As you doubtless remember, at Quebec last Summer the Staff people took a shot at drawing up terms of surrender for Italy. The American draft was short and to the point and was finally adopted and presented.

But later on the long and comprehensive terms, which were drawn up by your people, were presented to Badoglio.

I did not like them because they attempted to foresee every possibility in one document. But, as so often happens, when such an attempt is made, certain points were omitted and additional protocols with respect to naval and other questions had to be later presented.

That is a good deal the way I feel about all this detailed planning that we are jointly and severally making in regard to what we do when we get into France. I have been handed pages and pages with detailed instructions and appendices. I regard them as prophecies by prophets who cannot be infallible.

Therefore, I re-drew them with the thought of making the Commander-in-Chief solely responsible for Overlord and for the maintenance of law, order and reasonable justice for the first few months after we get into France. I

†From Roosevelt to Churchill, February 29, 1944, in U.S., Department of State, *FRUS, 1944* (Washington, D.C.: Government Printing Office, 1966), vol. 1, pp. 188-89.

have suggested that he get in touch with local persons and with representatives of the French National Committee in such places as they have military status, but that he and his staff bear the sole responsibility.

Now comes this business of what to do when we get into Germany. I understand that your Staff presented a long and comprehensive document—with every known kind of terms—to the European Advisory Commission, and that the Russians have done somewhat the same.

My people over here believe that a short document of surrender terms should be adopted. This, of course, has nothing to do with the locality of the occupying forces after they get into Germany, but it is an instrument of surrender which is in conformity with the general principles.

I am enclosing (a) an argument—facts bearing on the problem and (b) a proposed acknowledgment of unconditional surrender by Germany.

I hope much that you will read the argument. I think it is very cogent.

I am trying as hard as I can to simplify things—and sometimes I shudder at the thought of appointing as many new Committees and Commissions in the future as we have in the past!

I note that in the British proposal the territory of Germany is divided up in accordance with British plan. "Do please don't" ask me to keep any American forces in France. I just cannot do it! I would have to bring them all back home. As I suggested before, I denounce and protest the paternity of Belgium, France and Italy. You really ought to bring up and discipline your own children. In view of the fact that they may be your bulwark in future days, you should at least pay for their schooling now!

With my warm regards,
    As ever yours,

                              FRANKLIN D. ROOSEVELT

The two enclosures mentioned in the letter are not in the State Department or Roosevelt Library files, but can be found in the British archives; see Prime Minister's Operational Files (PREMIER 3)/file 197/folder 3/pp. 167-77, Public Record Office, London. The enclosures, relating to surrender terms for Germany, had been prepared by the Joint Chiefs of Staff.

8

American Plans for Occupying Germany

In this memo to the acting secretary of state, Edward Stettinius, Roosevelt clearly set forth his reasons for demanding that the American occupation zone in Germany be in the northwest, not the south. His reference to political considerations in the United States necessitating such a decision is obscure, but may have been a reference to the long-standing American belief that the British hoped to entangle the United States in European politics.

Document†

Memorandum for the Acting Secretary of State

I disagree with the British proposal of the demarcation of boundaries which would go into effect in Germany after their surrender or after fighting has stopped.

1. I do not want the United States to have the post-war burden of reconstituting France, Italy and the Balkans. This is not our natural task at a distance of 3,500 miles or more. It is definitely a British task in which the British are far more vitally interested than we are.

2. From the point of view of the United States, our principal object is not to take part in the internal problems in southern Europe but is rather to take part in eliminating Germany at a possible and even probable cost of a third World War.

3. Various points have been raised about the difficulties of transferring our troops, etc., from a French front to a northern German front—what is called a "leap-frog". These objections are specious because no matter where British and American troops are on the day of Germany's surrender, it is physically easy for them to go anywhere—north, east or south.

4. I have had to consider also the ease of maintaining American troops in some part of Germany. All things considered, and remembering that all supplies have to come 3,500 miles or more by sea, the United States should use the ports of northern Germany—Hamburg and Bremen—and the ports of the Netherlands for this long range operation.

†From: Memorandum from Roosevelt to Stettinius, February 21, 1944, U.S., Department of State Archives, Decimal File 740.00119 Control (Germany/-2-2144, National Archives, Washington, D.C.

5. Therefore, I think the American policy should be to occupy northwestern Germany, the British occupying the area from the Rhine south, and also being responsible for the policing of France and Italy, if this should become necessary.

6. In regard to the long range security of Britain against Germany, this is not a part of the first occupation. The British will have plenty of time to work that out, including Helgoland, air fields, etc. The Americans by that time will be only too glad to retire all their military forces from Europe.

7. If anything further is needed to justify this disagreement with the British lines of demarcation, I can only add that political considerations in the United States makes my decision conclusive.

You might speak to me about this if the above is not wholly clear.

F.D.R.

9

"Combined Directive for Military Government in Germany Prior to Defeat or Surrender"

Although CCS 551 theoretically pertained only to the interim period of occupation in Germany between a military takeover of portions of Germany and total surrender or occupation, it aimed American policy in directions which could and did make other decisions foregone conclusions. The directive established extensive autonomy for the military commanders and called for the restoration of coal and industrial production as required by the military. The clear emphasis was upon law, order, and a situation which would not produce civil unrest. Punishment of the Germans was limited to political rather than economic measures.

Document†

Combined Directive for Military Government in Germany Prior to Defeat or Surrender

April 28, 1944

1. This directive is subject to such alteration as may be necessary to meet joint recommendations of the European Advisory Commission in regard to the post-surrender period. It relates to the period before defeat or surrender of Germany and to such parts of Germany and Austria as are overrun by the forces under your command during such period. The same policy will be applied to occupied parts of Austria as to occupied parts of Germany except where different treatment is required for Austria to meet the provision of the Political Guide at Appendix B or other paragraphs dealing specifically with Austria.

†From: Combined Directive for Military Government in Germany Prior to Defeat or Surrender, Combined Chiefs of Staff 551, April 28, 1944, in *American Military Government,* ed. Hajo Holborn (Washington, D.C.: Infantry Journal Press, 1947), pp. 135-39, 143.

2. Military government will be established and will extend over all parts of Germany, including Austria, progressively as the forces under your command capture German territory. Your rights in Germany prior to unconditional surrender or German defeat will be those of an occupying power.

3. a. By virtue of your position you are clothed with supreme legislative, executive, and judicial authority and power in the areas occupied by forces under your command. This authority will be broadly construed and includes authority to take all measures deemed by you necessary, desirable or appropriate in relation to the exigencies of military operations and the objectives of a firm military government.

b. You are authorized at your discretion, to delegate the authority herein granted to you in whole or in part to members of your command, and further to authorize them at their discretion to make appropriate subdelegations. You are further authorized to appoint members of your command as Military Governors of such territory or areas as you may determine.

c. You are authorized to establish such military courts for the control of the population of the occupied areas as may seem to you desirable, and to establish appropriate regulations regarding their jurisdiction and powers.

d. The military government shall be a military administration which will show every characteristic of an Allied undertaking, acting in the interests of the United Nations. Whether or not U.S. and U.K. civil affairs personnel will be integrated other than at your headquarters will be a matter for your decision.

4. The U.S. and British flags shall be displayed at headquarters and posts of the military government. The administration shall be identical throughout those parts of Germany occupied by forces under your command, subject to any special requirements due to local circumstances.

5. The military administration shall contain no political agencies or political representatives of the U.S. and U.K. U.S. and U.K. political officers appointed at your headquarters will continue in office.

6. Representatives of civilian agencies of the U.S.-U.K. Governments or of UNRRA shall not participate unless and until you consider such participation desirable when it will be subject, as to time and extent, to decision by the Combined Chiefs of Staff on your recommendation. . . .

Political Guide

1. The administration shall be firm. It will at the same time be just and humane with respect to the civilian population so far as consistent with strict military requirements. You will strongly discourage fraternization between Allied troops and the German officials and population. It should be made clear to the local population that military occupation is intended; (1) to aid military operations; (2) to destroy Nazism-Fascism and the Nazi Hierarchy; (3) to maintain and preserve law and order; and (4) to restore normal conditions among the civilian population as soon as possible, insofar as such conditions will not interfere with military operations. . . .

6. The replacement of local Government officials who may be removed will rest with the Supreme Commander who will decide whether the functioning of the military government is better served by the appointment of officers of the occupation forces or by the use of the services of Germans. Military Government will be effected as a general principle through indirect rule. The principal link for this indirect rule should be at the Bezirk or Kreis level; controls at higher levels will be inserted at your discretion. Subject to any necessary dismissals, local officials should be instructed to continue to carry out their duties. No actual appointment of Germans to important posts will be made until it has been approved by the Combined Chiefs of Staff. It should be made clear to any German, after eventual appointment to an important post, and to all other Governmental officials and employees, that their continued employment is solely on the basis of satisfactory performance and behavior. In general the entire Nazi leadership will be removed from any post of authority and no permanent member of the German General Staff nor of the Nazi Hierarchy will occupy any important Governmental or Civil position. The German Supreme Command and General Staff will be disbanded in such a way as will insure that its possible resuscitation later will be made as difficult as possible. . . .

10. a. The propagation of Nazi doctrines and propaganda in any form shall be prohibited. Guidance on German education and schools will be given to you in a separate directive.

b. No political activity of any kind shall be countenanced unless authorized by you. Unless you deem otherwise, it is desirable that neither political personalities nor organized political groups, shall have any part in determining the policies of the military administration. It is essential to avoid any commitments to, or negotiations with, any political elements. German political leaders in exile shall have no part in the administration.

c. You will institute such censorship and control of press, printing, publications, and the dissemination of news or information by the above means and by mail, radio, telephone, and cable or other means as you consider necessary in the interests of military security and intelligence of all kinds and to carry out the principles laid down in this directive. . . .

The following directive relates to the period before the surrender of Germany. In areas where there are no military operations in progress, when practicable and consistent with military necessity you should:

(a) see that the systems of production, control, collection and distribution of food and agricultural produce are maintained, that food processing factories continue in operation and that the necessary labor and transport are provided to insure maximum production. German food and other supplies will be utilized for the German population to the minimum extent required to prevent disease and unrest. You will report on any surpluses that may be available as regards which separate instructions will be issued to you;

(b) instruct the German authorities to restore the various utilities to full working order, and to maintain coal mines in working condition and in full operation so far as transport will permit. Except insofar as their production is

needed to meet your requirements, or as you may be instructed in subsequent directives, munitions factories will be closed pending further instructions. You will be responsible for procuring such goods and materials for export as you may from time to time be directed to obtain for the use of the United Nations. You will take steps to insure that no sabotage or destruction is carried out by the Germans of any industrial plant, equipment or stocks, or of any books or records relating thereto. Pending the issue of further directives you will take such steps as you think desirable to preserve intact all such plant, equipment, books and records, paying particular attention to research and experimental establishment; . . .

10

The State Department on Germany and the World Economy

The State Department's long-term plans for Germany demonstrate its conception of the ideal postwar world. Although the proposals claimed to be compatible with demands for guarantees against future German aggression, the department's real emphasis was upon the rehabilitation of the German economy. To State Department planners, the war provided an unparalleled opportunity to redirect completely the economy of a major industrial nation toward a neomercantile relationship with the rest of the world; i.e., an interdependent system where production and consumption complement and supplement that of other nations rather than leading to cutthroat competition. Convinced that economic conflict invariably lay at the root of any military conflict, the State Department could honestly claim that its program would produce peace as well as prosperity.

Document†

I. The Relation Between American economic Policy with Respect to Germany and the Maintenance of Peace and Security

The basic long-term interest of the United States is peace. Consequently, so far as Germany is concerned, the basic objective of the United States is to see that country does not again disturb the peace.

Security against a renewal of German aggression must for the most part be achieved by means other than economic controls. Economic measures do not, and cannot by their nature, provide a substitute for the general international organization for the maintenance of international peace and security, and for other measures of security, to which the United States and its principal allies are pledged by the Moscow Declarations of October 1943. American economic policies with respect to Germany, as set forth below, are intended not to take the place of but to buttress the instrumentalities which will have primary responsibility for maintaining peace and security by helping to create conditions in the economic sphere which will remove the danger of future

†From Memorandum of the Executive Committee on Foreign Economic Policy, August 14, 1944, in U.S., Department of State, *FRUS*, 1944, vol. 1, pp. 279-85.

aggression on the part of Germany. On the one hand, they are intended to provide necessary safeguards against resumption by Germany of its pre-war policies of economic preparation for war. On the other hand, they are intended to create conditions under which Germany will contribute to the reconstruction of Europe and the development of a peaceful and expanding world economy in the benefits of which Germany can hope, in due course, to share. . . .

II. General Objectives and Methods

Within this framework, the over-all economic policy of the United States with respect to Germany is directed to the achievement of the following four major objectives:

1. The performance by Germany of acts of restitution and reparation required by the United Nations.

2. The control of Germany's economic war potential, by the conversion of German economic capacity directed to war purposes, and by rendering vulnerable to outside control the reconversion of Germany into a war economy able to launch and sustain a war of aggression.

3. The elimination of German economic domination in Europe, which Germany achieved by the systematic exploitation of the so-called "New Order" in Europe and by a series of other practices.

4. The effectuation in due time of a fundamental change in the organization and conduct of German economic life which will integrate Germany into the type of world economy envisaged by the Atlantic Charter.

III. Reconstitution or Maintenance of a
Minimum German Economy

The objectives just stated cannot be achieved unless the German economy is maintained at, or, if necessary, restored to at least a predetermined minimum level of effectiveness. The state of the German economy at the time of surrender and the attitude of the German people thereafter will have a decisive bearing on the nature and extent of the economic controls and measures which the occupation authorities will be able initially to put in force. Under the most favorable circumstances, economic disruption will be great. It is even possible that a more or less complete economic collapse will occur either before or after surrender. Such a collapse would delay or impair the effective operation of the economic controls proposed below. At least a minimum degree of operating effectiveness in the German economy is especially important not only to facilitate the achievement of the major long-run objectives stated above, but also

1. to facilitate an orderly demobilization and absorption of the German armed forces into peace-time occupations;

2. to facilitate the orderly return of Allied prisoners of war, foreign workers and other displaced persons to their countries of origin or choice;

3. to ensure the maintenance and safeguarding of property in Germany and elsewhere under German control, in which the United Nations, for any reason, have an interest;

4. to make possible prompt German contributions to the relief and rehabilitation of other countries;

5. to enforce, as far as possible, the economic rehabilitation of minority groups within Germany which have been systematically despoiled;

6. to make possible the early beginning of a program of restitution and reparation by Germany to other countries;

7. to facilitate the administration of the entire German inland transport. communication and power systems in the interests of the European economy as a whole;

8. to guarantee the prompt reorientation of forces and resources, after the defeat of Germany, from Europe to the Pacific for the defeat of Japan.

It is therefore essential that the occupation authorities should formulate and be in a position to enforce a series of economic and financial policies in Germany adequate to maintain or reconstitute a minimum German economy promptly. For this purpose Germany should be required initially to retain and place at the orders of the occupation authorities the administrative machinery charged with economic responsibility which may be in existence at the time of surrender. It is, further, essential to orderly reconversion to post-war production that preliminary programs be developed in advance of the military collapse of Germany for reparation deliveries to meet the immediate needs of claimant countries. . . .

IV. Restitution and Reparation

With regard to restitution, the major policy of this government is to require the return of identifiable stolen property to the governments of the former owners, and the relinquishment of German rights, claims, and controls over property in occupied countries obtained by duress or fraud.

The overriding principle with regard to reparation is that reparation policy should conform to the long-range objectives of this government respecting Germany and the world at large. Reparation cannot be regarded as a major means of accomplishing these objectives, but the effects of an unwise reparation settlement may go far toward defeating them. The reparation program must be designed so as to make the maximum contribution to the rehabilitation of the countries injured by German aggression, while at the same time avoiding or minimizing possible harm in other directions. . . .

V. Control of German Economic War Potential

It is the intention of this Government to pursue a policy with regard to German economic war potential which will reinforce and supplement the measures of strictly military disarmament which will be taken by the Allies after the unconditional surrender of Germany and which at the same time will be consistent with the major long-run economic objectives of the United States.

It is to be recognized that the pattern of the post-war German economy, and the steps to be taken in shaping it during the control period, will be influenced not only by policies relating to the German economic war potential, but also by policies relating to the reestablishment or maintenance of at least a minimum German economy in the control period, by policies relating to reparation and restitution, and by policies relating to the ultimate integration of Germany into a world economy. This section, which deals with the control of the German economic war potential, must therefore be read in connection with the other related sections of this paper.

Since a multitude of industries contribute to a country's economic war potential, the destruction, dismantling or conversion of plants producing arms, ammunition, or implements of war will eliminate only one aspect of this economic war potential. These military measures will be buttressed by strengthening the economies of Germany's neighbors under the program for restitution and reparation, and to eliminate those high-cost industries and agricultural activities which had been established in Germany to make it self-sufficient in terms of the requirements of a war economy. . . .

VI. Integration of Germany into the World Economy and the Elimination of German Economic Domination in Europe

A major objective of this Government with regard to Germany is that the latter must in due course be given the opportunity of finding a permanent place in the world economy, and of making a peaceful and constructive contribution to the development of the community of free nations envisaged by the Atlantic Charter. On the other hand, it is vital to prevent Germany from again becoming a primary focus of restrictive trade and financial practices. German economic self-sufficiency for war must be replaced by an economy which can be integrated into an inter-dependent world economy. . . .

11

The State Department on Reparations from Germany

The State Department's view of postwar reparations from Germany reflected its commitment to the speedy reintegration of that nation into the world economy. After complaining that reparations created an artificial pattern of trade, the following report on reparations calls for the quickest possible end to such payments so that Germany could again participate in multilateral trade. The department's pessimism about the chances of the wartime alliance surviving in the form of postwar cooperation shows in the recommendation of quick action at the United Nations aimed at implementing the American program before the coalition collapsed. Although the political atmosphere did not permit the State Department to flatly oppose reparations and harsh punishment for the Germans, that sentiment clearly prevailed with Hull and his advisors.

Document†

III. Résume of Recommendations on the Final Reparation Agreement

The essential elements of the program recommended in the Reparation Report may be summarized as follows:

1. *Time Period.*

The reparation period should begin as soon as the United Nations have the power to impose economic controls on Germany. It should be limited to a minimum of about five years from its inception but perhaps may have to be extended to ten. Both political and economic considerations emphasize the need for a short reparation period.

The urgent needs of the devastated areas for relief and rehabilitation and the desirability of restoring normally functioning economies in these areas as rapidly as possible demand quick and decisive action. Moreover, unless the United Nations stand ready to exploit fully the opportunity for cooperative action during the early period after the surrender of Germany, it may prove difficult to accomplish the aims of the program.

†From: Memorandum, Executive Committee on Foreign Economic Policy, August 12, 1944, in U.S., Department of State, *FRUS, 1944*, vol. 1, pp. 289-90.

The one-way movement of goods and services which takes place under reparation is artificial and necessarily different from normal trade. The longer it continues the longer is deferred the full resumption of regular multilateral trade and the desired integration of Germany into the world economy.

From the political point of view, it must be remembered that the humiliation and cost of reparation will almost inevitably be associated in the mind of the German public with the regime in power at the time. For this reason, long-continued reparation would prejudice the establishment of democratic government in Germany and, indirectly, the maintenance of peace.

The collection of substantial reparation from Germany will probably be impossible without fairly extensive controls over the German economy. Since this Government has taken the position that enduring controls of this nature are undesirable the length of the reparation period will need to be correspondingly limited.

It is realized, however, that the countries which have been devastated by Germany will probably demand a much longer reparation period. The long-range objectives of this Government make a five-year period preferable to a longer one. If it is found necessary to extend this period, however, reparation deliveries should in no event continue beyond ten years. In case a period in excess of five years is adopted, deliveries should taper off toward the end of the extended period. . . .

12

The British Foreign Office on Germany and Russia, August, 1944

Although British opinion was far from unanimous, Foreign Secretary Anthony Eden consistently supported a policy of promoting postwar cooperation with the Soviet Union. His conversations with Morgenthau during the latter's trip to England in August, 1944, show a willingness to punish Germany but a simultaneous insistence that policy toward Germany serve the interests of policy toward Russia. Morgenthau and his advisors did not present their views on the economic future of Germany but instead dealt primarily with the issue of partition. Eden's strong language about punishing Germany must, therefore, be understood in terms of support for dismemberment rather than pastoralization.

Document†

August 15, 1944

Conference at Sir Anthony Eden's Office at 4 P.M.

Present: Sir Anthony Eden
          Mr. W. Strang, British member of the EAC
          Secretary Morgenthau
          Ambassador Winant
          Mr. H.D. White

The conference had been arranged by Sir Anthony Eden on previous Sunday, who had suggested that if the Secretary could come to his office he could show him that portion of the Tehran conference dealing with the decision on partition of Germany.

Eden began by reading excerpts from a report on the Tehran conference. He said that the report had been prepared by Archibald Kerr and was sort of a telegraphic report and not a verbatim report. The gist of the excerpts which Eden read was as follows: President Roosevelt said that he would like to discuss the question of the partition of Germany. (At this point Eden explained parenthetically that Churchill had been pushing the Polish question

---

†From: H.D. White Memorandum for the Secretary's File of a Conference at Sir Anthony Eden's Office, August 18, 1944, Harry Dexter White Papers, Princeton University Library, Princeton, N.J. *

and that Stalin was trying to get away from it and he feared likewise President Roosevelt, but that Churchill kept trying to bring the Polish matter back into the discussion.) President Roosevelt said that Germany could be divided into three or fifteen parts. Stalin indicated smilingly that Churchill wasn't listening because he doubted whether Churchill was in favor of dividing Germany. Churchill replied that he hadn't yet left Lwow (thereby indicating that he still wanted to discuss the Polish question). The President expressed the view that the European Advisory Commission should be instructed to report on the problem of partitioning Germany. Stalin agreed. Since Stalin and Roosevelt felt strongly about the point Churchill said he was willing to agree that the Commission should examine and report on the question of the partition of Germany.

After Eden finished reading Secretary Morgenthau commented that the directive to the EAC to report on the partition of Germany apparently was not known to the technicians in the United States working on the problem of reparations because nothing in their memorandum suggested an awareness of that directive. . . .

Strange said that if Germany were divided it couldn't produce reparations. I replied that that might or might not be true, but in any case it raised the more important question as to whether or not the main objective of postwar policy toward Germany was to be obtaining reparations or some other more important objective. Eden heartily agreed and stressed the view that obtaining reparations was not the decisive consideration.

Strange said that it would be possible to deal much more effectively with a single Government in Germany during the early period and that therefore they (the British technicians) had proceeded on the assumption that there would be a unified Germany for the time being. I said that that might be true with respect to military disarmament, or even during the transition period, but the economic memorandum to which Strange was referring and the one being prepared by American technical committee dealt with reparations and long-term postwar policy. I said I didn't see how an economic memorandum could be intelligently prepared if it assumed that there was to be an undivided Germany whereas the policy decision according to which they were asked to draft a report called for a Germany divided into several or more parts. Eden agreed with that and Strange then said that they were also working out a memorandum based on the assumption of a divided Germany. I asked Winant if as a member of the EAC representing the United States he had ever instructed to go forward on a study based on the assumption tentatively decided upon at Tehran that Germany was to be separated into many parts. The Ambassador replied that he had been at Tehran and knew that decision had been made but that he didn't know how much he was supposed to tell to his own Department back home and that he had never received instructions from his own Department to work on such a proposal.

Secretary Morgenthau said that it was clear that the group in the State Department working on this problem were not informed that the report on an economic program for Germany during the postwar years was to be based on the assumption of a partitioned Germany. Secretary Morgenthau said when he went back to the States he would talk to President Roosevelt and Secretary Hull about the matter.

Eden said that Russia was watching this very closely and that if we were to make reparations and an undivided Germany a postwar policy that it would make Russia pursue a policy of her own. Eden said that there were some groups in both the United States and in England who feared that Communism would grow in Germany if a tough policy were pursued by the Allies. This group believed that it was important to have a strong Germany as protection against possible aggression by Russia. He said it was a question whether there was greater danger from a strong Germany or from a strong Russia. For his part he believed there was greater danger from a strong Germany. He asked Strange directly "Do you agree with me?" and Strange replied "I certainly do." . . .

Winant said that the President had told General Eisenhower that his supreme authority was to be in effect only to the end of hostilities. I remarked that there was a period of transition of several months after hostilities in which the Army would necessarily have control and that directives were being prepared for that period now. Those directives could be more intelligently drafted if the Army knew what the general objective was. If the general objective was to be divided their directives might be modified. Furthermore, the long-run objectives would in part be determined by what was done during the transition period and vice-versa. . . .

13

"We Have Got to be Tough with Germany…"

The Presidential Diaries in the Morgenthau papers (memoranda dictated by Morgenthau following his frequent meetings and regular luncheons with President Roosevelt) comprise one of the few records available of Roosevelt's private conversations on matters of policy. Morgenthau and the president were close friends, and their discussions were usually far more candid than most of Roosevelt's other policy meetings. Unfortunately, Morgenthau frequently read more into the president's remarks than Roosevelt apparently intended. Moreover, the president seems to have viewed such discussions as bull sessions with a friend rather than binding statements of policy. Nevertheless, when Morgenthau returned from England in August, 1944, and told Roosevelt of the state and war departments' planning for Germany, the president clearly adopted a hard-line attitude which ran counter to such plans. He reiterated his condemnations of the German people as a whole and clearly indicated that the southern zone of occupation in Germany posed no insurmountable problems.

Document†

I saw the President about twelve o'clock for half an hour. It was a very bad atmosphere to work under because he was half an hour late getting started, and I was told I would have only five minutes and then I could have the rest of the time on the train tonight. I stayed for a half hour but I couldn't do justice to my subject because I felt that I was under such pressure, and I talked terribly fast. The President was very attentive and tremendously interested and most friendly.

I told the President I had seen Churchill, who started the conversation by saying that England was broke. The President said, "What does he mean by that?" I said, "Yes, England really is broke." That seemed to surprise the President, and he kept coming back to it. I said that Churchill's attitude was that he was broke but not depressed about England's future. The President said that that was well put. He said, "What is his own attitude?" I said, "Well, he is going to tell Parliament about their financial condition at the right time

†From: Morgenthau Memorandum of Conversation With Roosevelt, August 19, 1944, Presidential Diaries, Morgenthau Papers, Franklin D. Roosevelt Library, Hyde Park, N.Y., pp. 1386-88.

after the Armistice, and that when he does that he is through." So the President said, "Oh, he is taking those tactics now. More recently his attitude was that he wanted to see England through the peace." . . .

During the course of the conversation, the President kept coming back to England's being broke. He said, "This is very interesting. I had no idea that England was broke. I will go over there and make a couple of talks and take over the British Empire." I told him how popular he was with the soldiers and how unpopular Churchill was. I told him about the difficulty of finding some one to take me through the shelters because both Churchill and Sir Robert Morris has been jeered when they went through them recently, and that finally they decided on Mrs. Churchill and Lady Mountbatten.

I then got on this question of the future of Germany, and I told him how little by little I put pieces together, and that finally Eden had read to me from the minutes of the Teheran Conference about Roosevelt, Churchill and Stalin agreeing to the dismemberment of Germany, and that as a result of that the European Advisory Committee had been set up. I said, "Mr. President, here in the State Department, under Hull, Pasvolsky has been making a study, but he didn't know about the Tehran Conference agreement." I told the President that when I called on Hull yesterday, Hull told me that he had never been told what was in the minutes at the Tehran meeting. The President didn't like it, but he didn't say anything. He looked very embarrassed, and I repeated it so that he would be sure to get it. I said that Pasvolsky couldn't get any instructions from Hull because Hull didn't know what had been agreed upon. I said, "as far as Winant goes, I can't quite understand it because he had a group study this, and Winant claims he knew what you did and still the group under him were not carrying out your instructions." I said, "I can't understand the English because Eden knew what happened because he said he was there and he had the minutes of the meeting, and still his man Strang, who represents England on the European Advisory Committee, had been making a study quite contrary to your wishes, and I think he lied because he said that they had begun a restudy a month ago. The sum and substance is that from the time of the Teheran Conference down to now nobody has been studying how to treat Germany roughly along the lines you wanted." The President said, "Give me thirty minutes with Churchill and I can correct this." Then the President said, "We have got to be tough with Germany and I mean the German people, not just the Nazis. You either have to castrate the German people or you have got to treat them in such a manner so they can't just go on reproducing people who want to continue the way they have in the past." I said, "Well, Mr. President, nobody is considering the question along those lines in Europe. In England they want to build up Germany so that she can pay reparations." He said, "What do we want reparations for?" He left no doubt in my mind that he and I are looking at this thing in the same way, but the people down the line arent. He used some example about Japan, showing how tough he is going to be. I said, "Mr. President, it is going to be the first three years that will count," and he agreed.

I told the President about my talk with Eisenhower, who is perfectly prepared to be tough with the Germans when he first goes in, but I said that all the plans in G-5 are contrary to that view. They are going to treat them like a WPA project.

I again want to say that the thing that seemed to bother the President was not so much that the people down the line were not studying to be tough with the Germans as it was that England was broke, although he left no doubt whatsoever in my mind that he personally wants to be tough with the Germans. He said, "They have been tough with us."

I then told him that the Army, contrary to what I thought his wishes were, were planning to put the United States Army into the south of Germany, and he said that that was unimportant. He said the only thing he cared about was that he didn't want to be left with France in his lap. . . .

14

"Handbook of Military Government for Germany"

Morgenthau and his staff believed that War Department planning for the military occupation of Germany set in motion steps which would inevitably lead to the economic rehabilitation of that nation. Moreover, those plans assumed Allied responsibility for the quality of life in Germany, something Morgenthau claimed would result in the Germans suffering less than those they had conquered. The following summary of the army guide for occupation authorities prepared the way for Morgenthau to argue that the Germans should be left completely to their own devices with Allied controls being only negative; i.e., disarmament and deindustrialization. Clearly, the army hoped to avoid political questions and concentrated instead on law, order, and efficiency.

Document†

The following are extracts from the "Handbook of Military Government for Germany", to be given for guidance to every U.S. and U.K. military government officer entering Germany. They tend to indicate the type of thinking and planning upon which the program of military government for Germany is being formulated. The "Handbook" is based on and is in harmony with the economic and political directives approved by the Combined Civil Affairs Committee under the authority of the Combined Chiefs of Staff.

"Your main and immediate task, to accomplish your mission, is to get things running, to pick up the pieces, to restore as quickly as possible the official functioning of the German civil government in the area for which you are responsible.... The first concern of military government will be to see that the machine works and works efficiently".

"The principles with which Officers in Military Government Staffs and Detachments will be concerned include: the reorganization of the German Police and the maintenance of Law and Order; the supervision of the German Judiciary and the establishment of Allied Military Courts; the control of the German Finances; the protection of property; the establishment and

---

†From: Morgenthau, Memorandum for the President, August 25, 1944, Presidential Diaries, Morgenthau Papers, Roosevelt Library, pp. 1394-96.

maintenance of an adequate standard of public health; the promotion of agriculture; the control, supply and distribution of food and essential supplies of every kind; the restoration and maintenance of public utilities; the provision for the gradual rehabilitation of peacetime industry and a regulated economy; the employment of Labour and the prevention of industrial unrest. . . ."

"Military Government Officers will, in conjunction with other interested and affected agencies and authorities, ensure that steps are taken to:
(1) Import needed commodities and stores.
(2) Convert industrial plants from war to consumer goods production.
(3) Subsidize essential economic activities where necessary.
(4) Reconstruct German foreign trade with priority for the needs of the United Nations.
(5) Modify existing German regulations controlling industrial and raw material production."

"The highly centralized German administrative system is to be retained unless otherwise directed by higher authority".

"All existing German regulations and ordinances relating to . . .production, supply or distribution will remain in force until specifically amended or abrogated. Except as otherwise indicated by circumstances or directed by higher authority, present German production and primary processing of fuels, ores and other raw materials will be maintained at present levels".

"The food supply will be administered so as to provide, if possible, a diet on the basis of an overall average of 2000 calories per day. Members of the German forces will be rated as normal consumers. The control of retail prices will be continued. The existing rationing system and classification of consumer groups will be maintained subject to modifications required by circumstances. . . . Should the indigenous products of Germany be insufficient to provide such a basic ration, the balance will be made up by imports".

"All possible steps will be taken to ensure the utilization of German economic, material and industrial facilities to an extent necessary to provide such raw materials, goods, supplies or services as are required for military and essential civilian needs, and to any additional extent—as approved by higher authority—necessary to provide surpluses for international transfer, supplies for reparational requisition, and legitimate industrial stock-piling".

"The fishing industry has long been important in German economy, but owing to the requisitioning of trawlers for naval operations, the most important North Sea fish catch has been seriously curtailed. Before extensive commercial fishing can be resumed, a considerable amount of fishing gear will be required as well as stores and material for the repair and reconditioning of fishing vessels. There will possibly also be an immediate shortage of fuel and lubricants".

"The Agricultural economy will be freed of Nazi discrimination. It will not otherwise be changed except where direct advantages are to be gained. Agricultural production control, and grain and other agricultural products collection agencies existing prior to occupation will be maintained or re-established. Equitable prices co-ordinated at Reich level will be fixed for farm products. Violations of farm price control, wages or rationing regulations will be severely punished".

"The main objective of Allied Military Government in the financial field is to take such temporary measures as will attempt to minimize the potential financial disorder and chaos that is likely to occur and thus assist the military forces in their operations and ease the burdens that will face the more permanent Allied Control organization that will later deal with the problems of Germany".

"Wherever possible, removals and appointments (of civil servants) will be made by Military Government officers acting through German officials who are vested with this authority under German law; nothing will be done which would unnecessarily disturb the regular German civil service procedure or deprive the official or employee to be removed of any ultimate rights to which he may be justifiably entitled under German law, after cessation of military government".

"International boundaries will be deemed to be as they were on 31 December 1937".

15

The Morgenthau Plan for Germany

This and the following document together summarize the Morgenthau Plan for Germany. Although the Morgenthau Plan is frequently labeled merely a program for the pastoralization of Germany, it is clearly much more than just that. Educational and political reform through punishment and partition lay at the heart of Morgenthau's proposals.

Document†

Suggested Post-Surrender Program for Germany

1. *Demilitarization of Germany*

It should be the aim of the Allied Forces to accomplish the complete demilitarization of Germany in the shortest possible period of time after surrender. This means completely disarming the German Army and people (including the removal or destruction of all war material), the total destruction of the whole German armament industry, and the removal or destruction of other key industries which are basic to military strength.

2. *Partitioning of Germany*

(a) Poland should get that part of East Prussia which doesn't go to the U.S.S.R. and the southern portion of Silesia as indicated on the attached map. . . .

(b) France should get the Saar and the adjacent territories bounded by the Rhine and the Moselle Rivers.

(c) As indicated in part 3 an International Zone should be created containing the Ruhr and the surrounding industrial areas.

(d) The remaining portion of Germany should be divided into two autonomous, independent states, (1) a South German state comprising Bavaria, Wuerttemberg, Baden and some smaller areas and (2) a North German state comprising a large part of the old state of Prussia, Saxony, Thuringia and several smaller states.

There shall be a custom union between the new South German state and Austria, which will be restored to her pre-1938 political borders.

†From: Morgenthau, Memorandum to the President, "Suggested Post-Surrender Program for Germany," September 5, 1944, in U.S., Department of State, *FRUS, Quebec, 1944,* pp. 101-106.

3. *The Ruhr Area*

(The Ruhr, surrounding industrial areas, as shown on the attached map, including the Rhineland, the Kiel Canal, and all German territory north of the Kiel Canal.)

Here lies the heart of German industrial power, the caldron of wars. This area should not only be stripped of all presently existing industries but so weakened and controlled that it can not in the foreseeable future become an industrial area. The following steps will accomplish this:

(*a*) Within a short period, if possible not longer than 6 months after the cessation of hostilities, all industrial plants and equipment not destroyed by military action shall either be completely dismantled and removed from the area or completely destroyed. All equipment shall be removed from the mines and the mines shall be thoroughly wrecked.

It is anticipated that the stripping of this area would be accomplished in three stages:

(*i*) The military forces immediately upon entry into the area shall destroy all plants and equipment which cannot be removed.

(*ii*) Removal of plants and equipment by members of the United Nations as restitution and reparation (Paragraph 4).

(*iii*) All plants and equipment not removed within a stated period of time, say 6 months, will be completely destroyed or reduced to scrap and allocated to the United Nations.

(*b*) All people within the area should be made to understand that this area will not again be allowed to become an industrial area. Accordingly, all people and their families within the area having special skills or technical training should be encouraged to migrate permanently from the area and should be as widely dispersed as possible.

(*c*) The area should be made an international zone to be governed by an international security organization to be established by the United Nations. In governing the area the international organization should be guided by policies designed to further the above stated objectives.

4. *Restitution and Reparation*

Reparations, in the form of recurrent payments and deliveries, should not be demanded. Restitution and reparation shall be effected by the transfer of existing German resources and territories, e.g.,

(*a*) by restitution of property looted by the Germans in territories occupied by them:

(*b*) by transfer of German territory and German private rights in industrial property situated in such territory to invaded countries and the international organization under the program of partition:

(*c*) by the removal and distribution among devastated countries of industrial plants and equipment situated within the International Zone and the North and South German states delimited in the section on partition;

(*d*) by forced German labor outside Germany; and

(*e*) by confiscation of all German assets of any character whatsoever outside of Germany.

5. *Education and Propaganda*

(*a*) All schools and universities will be closed until an Allied   Commission of Education has formulated an effective reorganization program. It is contemplated that it may require a considerable period of time before any institutions of higher education are reopened. Meanwhile the education of German students in foreign universities will not be prohibited. Elementary schools will be reopened as quickly as appropriate teachers and textbooks are available.

(*b*) All German radio stations and newspapers, magazines, weeklies, etc. shall be discontinued until adequate controls are established and an appropriate program formulated.

6. *Political Decentralization*

The military administration in Germany in the initial period should be carried out with a view toward the eventual partitioning of Germany into three states. To facilitate partitioning and to assure its permanence the military authorities should be guided by the following principles:

(*a*) Dismiss all policy-making officials of the Reich government and deal primarily with local governments.

(*b*) Encourage the reestablishment of state governments in each of the states (*Länder*) corresponding to 18 states into which Germany is presently divided and in addition make the Prussian provinces separate states.

(*c*) Upon the partition of Germany, the various state governments should be encouraged to organize a federal government for each of the newly partitioned areas. Such new governments should be in the form of a confederation of states, with emphasis on states' rights and a large degree of local autonomy.

7. *Responsibility of Military for Local German Economy*

The sole purpose of the military in control of the German economy shall be to facilitate military operations and military occupation. The Allied Military Government shall not assume responsibility for such economic problems as price controls, rationing, unemployment, production, reconstruction, distribution, consumption, housing, or transportation, or take any measures designed to maintain or strengthen [the German economy, except those which are essential to military] operations. The responsibility for sustaining the German economy and people rests with the German people with such facilities as may be available under the circumstances.

8. *Controls Over Development of German Economy*

During a period of at least twenty years after surrender adequate controls, including controls over foreign trade and tight restrictions on capital imports, shall be maintained by the United Nations designed to prevent in the Newly-established states the establishment or expansion of key industries basic to the German military potential and to control other key industries.

9. *Punishment of War Crimes and Treatment of Special Groups*

There is attached (Appendix B) a program for the punishment of certain war crimes and for the treatment of Nazi organizations and other special groups.

10. *Wearing of Insignia and Uniforms*

(*a*) No person in German[y] (except members of the United Nations and neutral countries) shall be permitted to wear any military insignia of rank or branch of service, service ribbons or military medals.

(*b*) No such person shall be permitted to wear, after 6 months from the cessation of hostilities any military uniform or any uniform of any quasi military organizations.

11. *Prohibition on Parades*

No military parades shall be permitted anywhere in German[y] and all military bands shall be disbanded.

12. *Aircraft*

All aircraft (including gliders), whether military or commercial will be confiscated for later disposition. No German shall be permitted to operate or to help operate such aircraft, including those owned by foreign interests.

13. *United States Responsibility*

(*a*) The responsibility for the execution of the post-surrender program for Germany set forth in this memorandum is the joint responsibility of the United Nations. The execution of the joint policy agreed upon should therefore eventually be entrusted to the international body which emerges from United Nations discussions.

Consideration of the specific measures to be taken in carrying out the joint program suggests the desirability of separating the task to be performed during the initial period of military occupation from those which will require a much longer period of execution. While the U.S., U.K. and U.S.S.R. will, for practical reasons, play the major role (of course aided by the military forces of other United Nations) in demilitarizing Germany (point 1) the detailed execution of other parts of the program can best be handled by Germany's continental neighbors.

(*b*) When Germany has been completely demilitarized there would be the following distribution of duties in carrying out the German program:

(*i*) The U.S. would have military and civilian representation on whatever international commission or commissions may be established for the execution of the whole German program and such representatives should have adequate U.S. staffs.

(*ii*) The primary responsibility for the policing of Germany and for civil administration in Germany would be assumed by the military forces of Germany's continental neighbors. Specifically these should include Russian, French, Polish, Czech, Greek, Yugoslav, Norwegian, Dutch and Belgian soldiers.

(*c*) Under this program United States troops could be withdrawn within a relatively short time. Actual withdrawal of United States troops should not precede agreement with the U.S.S.R. and the U.K. on the principles set forth in this memorandum. . . .

Appendix B

Punishment of Certain War Crimes and Treatment of Special Groups

A. *Punishment of Certain War Criminals*

(1) *Arch-criminals.*

A list of the arch-criminals of this war whose obvious guilt has generally been recognized by the United Nations shall be drawn up as soon as possible and transmitted to the appropriate military authorities. The military authorities shall be instructed with respect to all persons who are on such list as follows:

(a) They shall be apprehended as soon as possible and identified as soon as possible after apprehension, the identification to be approved by an officer of the General rank.

(b) When such identification has been made the person identified shall be put to death forthwith by firing squads made up of soldiers of the United Nations. . . .

16

The Morgenthau Plan: Preventing a World War III

Just prior to the president's departure for the 1944 Quebec Conference with Churchill, the Treasury Department sent Roosevelt a briefing book on postwar planning for Germany. Although it repeated much of the earlier material in Morgenthau's September 5 memorandum (see Document 15), it did elaborate extensively on the questions of economic planning and reform of the German character. Morgenthau's emphasis on the benefits his plan would give to Great Britain not only fit in with Roosevelt's desires but also reflected Morgenthau's intention to build up Germany's neighbors.

Document†

Reparations Mean a Powerful Germany

If we were to expect Germany to pay recurring reparations, whether in the form of money or goods, we would be forced at the very beginning to start a rehabilitation and reconstruction program for the German economy. For instance, we would have to supply her with transportation equipment, public utility repairs, food for her working population, machinery for heavy industry damaged by bombing, reconstruction of housing and industrial raw materials. No matter how the program would be dressed up, we would, in effect be doing for Germany what we expect to do for the liberated areas of Europe but perhaps on an even greater scale, because of Germany's more advanced industrialization.

When reparation deliveries cease Germany will be left with a more powerful economy and a larger share of foreign markets than she had in the Thirties. . . .

It is a Fallacy That Europe Needs a Strong Industrial Germany

1. The assumption sometimes made that Germany is an indispensable source of industrial supplies for the rest of Europe is not valid.

U.S., U.K. and the French-Luxembourg-Belgian industrial group could easily have supplied out of unused industrial capacity practically all that

†From: U.S., Treasury Department, "Program to Prevent Germany from Starting a World War III," September 9, 1944, in U.S., Department of State, *FRUS, Quebec, 1944*, pp. 131-40.

Germany supplied to Europe during the pre-war period. In the post-war period the expanded industrial capacity of the United Nations, particularly the U.S., can easily provide the reconstruction and industrial needs of Europe without German assistance. . . .

5. In short, the statement that a healthy European economy is dependent upon German industry was never true, nor will it be true in the future. Therefore the treatment to be accorded to Germany should be decided upon without reference to the economic consequences upon the rest of Europe. At the worst, these economic consequences will involve relatively minor economic disadvantages in certain sections of Europe. At best, they will speed up the industrial development of Europe outside of Germany. But any disadvantages will be more than offset by real gains to the political objectives and the economic interests of the United Nations as a whole. . . .

How British Industry Would Benefit by Proposed Program

1. *The British coal industry would recover from its thirty year depression* by gaining new markets. Britain would meet the major portion of the European coal needs formerly met by the annual Ruhr production of 125 million tons. The consequent expansion of British coal output would allow for the development of a coherent program for the expansion and reorganization of what has been Britain's leading depressed industry since 1918 and facilitate the elimination of the depressed areas.

2. *The reduction in German industrial capacity would eliminate German competition with British exports* in the world market. Not only will England be in a position to recapture many of the foreign markets she lost to Germany after 1918, but she will participate in supplying the devastated countries of Europe with all types of consumer and industrial goods for their reconstruction needs in the immediate post-war years.

3. *Transference of a large section of German shipping,* both commercial and naval, and shipbuilding equipment to England will be an important item in England's program of post-war economic expansion of restitution.

4. *Britain's foreign exchange position will be strengthened* and the pressure on sterling reduced by the expansion of her exports and shipping services.

5. *The assurance of peace and security* would constitute England's greatest single economic benefit from the proposed program designed to put Germany in a position never again to wage effective war on the continent. England would be able to undertake the program for economic and social reconstruction advanced in the Beveridge plan and the Government program for full employment without having to worry about the future financial burdens of maintaining [a] large army and huge armament industries indefinitely.

6. *Britain's political stability would be reinforced* by her increased ability to meet the insistent domestic demands for economic reform resulting from the assurances of security and of an expansion of her exports.

[Section 7]

The Well-Being of the German Economy is the Responsibility of the Germans and Not of the Allied Military Authorities

The economic rehabilitation of Germany is the problem of the German people and not of the Allied Military authorities. The German people must bear the consequences of their own acts. . . .

What To Do About German Education

The militaristic spirit which pervades the German people has been deliberately fostered by all educational institutions in Germany for many decades. Schools, Colleges and Universities were used with great effectiveness to instill into the children and the youth of the nation the seeds of aggressive nationalism and the desire for world domination. Re-education of the German people must hence be part of the program to render Germany ineffective as an aggressive power.

Re-education cannot be effectively undertaken from outside the country and by teachers from aborad. It must be done by the Germans themselves. The hard facts of defeat and of the need for political, economic and social reorientation must be the teachers of the German people. The existing educational system which is utterly nazified must be completely reorganized and reformed. The chief task will be to locate politically reliable teachers and to educate, as soon as possible, new teachers who are animated by a new spirit. . . .

German Militarism Cannot be Destroyed by Destroying Nazism Alone

(1) *The Nazi regime is essentially the culmination of the unchanging German drive toward aggression.*

(*a*) German society has been dominated for at least three generations by powerful forces fashioning the German state and nation into a machine for military conquest and self-aggrandizement. Since 1864 Germany has launched five wars of aggression against other powers, each war involving more destruction over larger areas than the previous one.

(*b*) As in the case of Japan, the rapid evolution of a modern industrial system in Germany immeasurably strengthened the economic base of German militarism without weakening the Prussian feudal ideology or its hold on German society.

(*e*) The Nazi regime is *not* an excrescence on an otherwise healthy society but an organic growth out of the German body politic. Even before the Nazi regime seized power, the German nation had demonstrated an unequalled capacity to be seduced by a militarist clique offering the promise of economic security and political domination in exchange for disciplined acceptance of its leadership. What the Nazi regime has done has been to systematically debauch the passive German nation on an unprecedented scale and shape it into an organized and dehumanized military machine integrated by all the forces of modern technique and science. . . .

17

Convincing Roosevelt

Discussions within the Cabinet Committee on Postwar Germany (consisting of Hull, Morgenthau, Stimson, and Hopkins) illustrate Roosevelt's concensus approach to decision-making. Since only Stimson expressed any opposition to Morgenthau's proposals, the president could follow his personal inclination to punish the German nation. Nevertheless, he made no firm commitments but only expressed general agreement with the idea of an agrarian Germany. Roosevelt's concern for the effect any agreement would have on Soviet attitudes again indicates his priorities. Although this conversation occurred before the president had fully examined either the Morgenthau Plan or Stimson's objections to it (see Document 18), the discussion shows that Morgenthau's efforts since August, 1944 had been quite successful.

Document†

I saw the President, and Stimson started right in and he had these two memos which he gave the President (copies attached). I think he said they were his answers to my memorandum and to Hull's memorandum.

I then gave them each a copy of our memorandum, and the President tried his best to read it and seemed very much interested.

Hopkins brought up the question of partition and seemed to be the devil's advocate for it. Stimson has been talking to Bowman who is against partition. The President said that he would go along with the idea of the trusteeship for the Ruhr, the Saar and the Kiel Canal. The President also said that he is in favor of dividing Germany into three parts. Hopkins kept pressing the point about partitioning Germany, and I frankly don't know where he stands. Hopkins said to the President, "Would it be correct to define your position as saying you inclined toward partition?" and the President said, "Yes," but he is in favor of doing it now and not waiting.

During the discussion, Stimson said that we must get along with Russia.

The President kept looking through the book and wanted to know whether I had the part put in about uniforms and marching, and I said that it was in there. The President read out loud No. 4, "It is a fallacy that Europe needs a strong industrial Germany." The President said, "This is the first time I have seen this stated." He said that everybody seems to disagree on that point, but he said "I agree with this idea." He said, "Furthermore, I believe in an agricultural Germany." (I evidently made a real impression on the

†From: Morgenthau, Memorandum of a Conversation with Hull, Roosevelt, Stimson, and Hopkins, September 9, 1944, Presidential Diary, Morgenthau Papers, Roosevelt Library, pp. 1431-32.

President the time he came to my house, and the more I talk to him the more I find that he seems to be coming around to our viewpoint.) . . .

The President put up this question, "Supposing the Russians want to insist on reparations, and the English and the United States don't want any, what happens then?" So I spoke up and said, "Well, my experience with the Russians at Bretton Woods was that they were very intelligent and reasonable, and I think that if the matter is put to them about reparations, that there is a good chance of their going on with us, provided we offer them something in lieu thereof."

As a result of this conference, I am very much more encouraged, and if I could only have a chance to talk with the President alone I think I could get somewhere.

I kept saying, "Don't you want this committee to draft for you a suggestion for the American policy towards Germany?" I said it a couple of times and got nowhere, and then Hull said that he had sent some paper on the economic future of Germany to Stimson, and he had not heard from Stimson. Stimson said he didn't know what he was talking about.

Hull just won't get in on the discussion, and just what his game is I don't know. As I came in, the President was asking Hull whether he didn't want to come to Quebec, and Hull said he was too tired. At the beginning of the discussion the President said, "Well, I think there will be two things brought up at Quebec. One is the military and the other is the monetary because Churchill keeps saying he is broke," and the President said, "If they bring up the financial situation, I will want Henry to come up to Quebec." This is the second time he has said that.

18

Opposition to the Plan

The primary opposition to the Morgenthau Plan came from Secretary of War Stimson. Firmly convinced that a punitive peace would only create resentment and the conditions for yet another conflict with Germany, he also claimed that the pastoralization of Germany by force would violate all the principles which the United States had fought for. Stimson placed the blame for Germany's conduct on the Nazis, not the general public; his recommendations therefore fundamentally differed from those of Morgenthau. He also believed that Germany's industrial production could materially assist in the rehabilitation of all Europe and that the destruction of those industries was foolish. To Stimson, the war was simply another chapter in the history of world power politics. To Morgenthau, the war demonstrated the moral degeneracy of all Germans and provided an opportunity to institute permanent reforms in that land.

Document†

Memorandum by the Secretary of War (Stimson)

Washington, September 9, 1944.

Secret

Our discussions relate to a matter of method entirely; our objective is the same. It is not a question of a soft treatment of Germany or a harsh treatment of Germany. We are all trying to devise protection against recurrence by Germany of her attempts to dominate the world. We differ as to method. The fundamental remedy of Mr. Morgenthau is to provide that the industry of Germany shall be substantially obliterated. Although expressed only in terms of the Ruhr, the fact of the matter is that the Ruhr and the adjacent territories which Mr. Morgenthau would include in his program constitute, particularly after the amputations that are proposed, the core of German industry. His proposition is

"the total destruction of the whole German armament industry and the removal or destruction of other key industries which are basic to military strength."

In speaking of the Ruhr and surrounding industrial areas, he says: "This area should not only be stripped of all presently existing industries but so weakened and controlled that it cannot in the foreseeable future become an industrial area—all industrial plants and equipment not destroyed by military

†From: Stimson, Memorandum to the President, September 9, 1944, in U.S., Department of State, *FRUS, Quebec, 1944*, pp. 123-26.

action shall either be completely dismantled ore removed from the area or completely destroyed, all equipment shall be removed from the mines and the mines shall be thoroughly wrecked."

I am unalterably opposed to such a program for the reasons given in my memorandum dated Septemver 5 which is already before the President. I do not think that the reasons there stated need again be elaborated. In substance, my point is that these resources constitute a natural and necessary asset for the productivity of Europe. In a period when the world is suffering from destruction and from want of production, the concept of the total obliteration of these values is to my mind wholly wrong. My insistence is that these assets be conserved and made available for the benefit of the whole of Europe, including particularly Great Britain. The internationalization of the Ruhr or the trusteeship of its products—I am not prepared at the moment to discuss details of method—constitutes a treatment of the problem in accord with the needs and interests of the world. To argue that we are incapable of sustained effort to control such wealth within proper channels is to destroy any hope for the future of the world. I believe that the education furnished us by the Germans in two world wars, plus the continuity of interest which such a trusteeship would stimulate is sufficient insurance that we can be trusted to deal with the problem. The unnatural destruction of this industry would, on the other hand, be so certain, in my judgment, to provoke sympathy for the Germans that we would create friends both in this country and abroad for the Germans, whereas now most of the peoples of the world are thoroughly antipathetic to them.

The other fundamental point upon which I feel we differ is the matter of the trial and punishment of those Germans who are responsible for crimes and depredations. Under the plan proposed by Mr. Morgenthau, the so-called arch-criminals shall be put to death by the military without provision for any trial and upon mere identification after apprehension. The method of dealing with these and other criminals requires careful thought and a well-defined procedure. Such procedure must embody, in my judgment, at least the rudimentary aspects of the Bill of Rights, namely, notification to the accused of the charge, the right to be heard and, within reasonable limits, to call witnesses in his defense. I do not mean to favor the institution of state trials or to introduce any cumbersome machinery but the very punishment of these men in a dignified manner consistent with the advance of civilization, will have all the greater effect upon posterity. Furthermore, it will afford the most effective way of making a record of the Nazi system of terrorism and of the effort of the Allies to terminate the system and prevent its recurrence.

I am disposed to believe that at least as to the chief Nazi officials, we should participate in an international tribunal constituted to try them. They should be charged with offences against the laws of the Rules of War in that they have committed wanton and unnecessary cruelties in connection with the prosecution of the war. This law of the Rules of War has been upheld by our own Supreme Court and will be the basis of judicial action against the Nazis.

Even though these offences have not been committed against our troops, I feel that our moral position is better if we take our share in their conviction. Other war criminals who have committed crimes in subjugated territory should be returned in accordance with the Moscow Declaration to those territories for trial by national military commissions having jurisdiction of the offence under the same Rules of War. I have great difficulty in finding any means whereby military commissions may try and convict those responsible for excesses committed within Germany both before and during the war which have no relation to the conduct of the war. I would be prepared to construe broadly what constituted a violation of the Rules of War but there is a certain field in which I fear that external courts cannot move. Such courts would be without jurisdiction in precisely the same way that any foreign court would be without jurisdiction to try those who were guilty of, or condoned, lynching in our own country.

The above are the two main points with which I differ from the proposed program submitted by the Secretary of the Treasury.

Partition

I have an open mind on partition and although I have given the matter substantial consideration I have, as yet, come to no conclusion as to wisdom or method of partition. I feel we cannot deal effectively with that subject until we have had an interchange of views with the English and the Russians. I, myself, seek further light on this subject. I, certainly, would not discourage any spontaneous effort toward separation of the country into two or more groups.

Amputation

I understand that there is some general recognition of the probability of Russia or the Poles taking East Prussia and some parts of Silesia. I suggest that we interpose no objection to this but that we take no part in the administration of the area. On the Western border the primary question is the matter of dealing with the Ruhr but it has also been suggested that the Rhineland the the Saar be delivered to France. Naturally I am in favor of the automatic return of Alsace and Lorraine to France but though my mind is not irrevocably closed against it, I feel that the burden proof lies on those who suggest giving France more territory. She will come out of this war with her Empire practically intact, with a reduced population and already possessing a very valuable bit of ore in the Longwy-Briey area. To give her a substantial territory of German-speaking and German-bred people would create another problem in the balance of Europe. To counteract this, I would give France a share in the benefits of the internationalization of the Saar and the Ruhr and the advantage which this gives of what would in effect be an international barrier between France and Germany.

There are certain other methods of punishment affecting the personal lives of individual Germans proposed by the Secretary of the Treasury to which I am opposed as constituting irritations of no fundamental value and, indeed, of considerable danger, but these are primarily matters of administration which I think need not be discussed at this time. In some part, at least, they had best be determined by those who have the primary responsibility for the administration of the occupation.

As a suggestion, I propose that during the interim period, which is all that we can deal with at the moment, the President be recommended to approve a program generally in accord with the memorandum submitted by the Secretary of State at the meeting of the Cabinet Committee on Tuesday, September 5, except for a modification of subparagraph 2 (h) of that memorandum and certain other additions on which I hope we can all agree, which suggested changes I append hereto.

19

Harry Hopkins on Germany, September, 1944

The British regularly overestimated the influence and role of Harry Hopkins on American policy, particularly later in the war (1944-45) when Adm. William Leahy and James F. Byrnes took his place Roosevelt's major personal advisors. Hopkins's desire to be the occupation governor of Germany may have contributed to his apparent opposition to partition, but he clearly agreed with Morgenthau's overall program for achieving security via a reorientation of the German economy and society. Hopkins's vague statements only contributed to British uncertainty about American policy.

Document†

I had a desultory talk two nights ago with Harry [Hopkins], Sir A. Cadogan also present. Harry developed some very tentative ideas about the treatment of Germany. He began by saying the drift of opinion here was against partition; there might well be difficulties about prolonged military occupation, not the least of which in his views was the certain development of fraternization, and he had therefore been turning over the possibilities of getting the security we all wanted through economic means. These were pretty vague, and ranged from physical destruction of the Ruhr heavy industry, to the keeping of all Germans indefinitely on a planned and national economy.

2. He said that urgent thought was being turned on to these subjects here and you may like to know direction in which his mind is moving.

†From: Halifax to the Foreign Office, September 7, 1944, FO 371/39080/4010, paper C11900, Public Record Office, London.

20

The British Foreign Office on Germany and Russia, September, 1944

The historic concern of the British Foreign Office regarding the role of Russia in any European political equation characterized its consideration of plans for postwar Germany. When a Foreign Office paper, written in early September, 1944, sharply criticized the military's tendency to think in terms of an anti-Soviet bloc, Foreign Minister Eden strongly supported the paper. Although Churchill remained doubtful, the Foreign Office steadfastly supported policies which would help preserve the cooperative atmosphere created by the wartime alliance with the Soviet Union. Nevertheless, British officials tended to make postwar planning for Germany a function of postwar planning for relations with Russia.

Document†

VII. Anglo-Russian Relations

31. The question that raises the greatest difficulty is the effect of dismemberment on our relations with the Soviet Union. It can be considered from two points of view, (a) as a possible source of dispute and (b) as an insurance against Russian aggression.

32. The second point may be considered first, as the Chiefs of Staff lay emphasis on the strategic advantage that would ensue from dismemberment as an insurance against the possibility of an eventually hostile U.S.S.R. The argument seems to be that dismemberment could be used to keep Germany prostrate just for so long as it might serve our purpose, and that at a given moment we could suddenly reverse our policy and find in Western Germany a reliable ally prepared to reinforce our war potential and to join us in battle against a combination of the strongest military power in Europe and follow Germans in the East. Such a suggestion seems little less than fantastic. But it is worse than that. It is playing with fire. The policy of His Majesty's Government is to preserve the unity and collaboration of the United Nations. If we start preparing our post-war plans with the idea at the back of our

†From: Armistice and Post-War Committee, "The Dismemberment of Germany," September 10, 1944, Foreign Office 371/39080/4010, Public Records Office, London.

minds that the Germans may serve as part of an anti-Soviet bloc, we shall quickly destroy any hope of preserving the Anglo-Soviet Alliance and soon find ourselves advocating relaxations of the disarmament and other measures which we regard as essential guarantees against future German aggression. This is not only a matter of strategy. It is a matter of high policy.

33. The question then arises whether dismemberment is likely to give rise to friction with the Soviet Government. This is not easy to answer because we do not know if they will advocate dismemberment or not. It is true that at Teheran Marshal Stalin advocated the division of Germany into smallish pieces and the use of force, if necessary, to prevent their re-uniting. Against this we have M. Gousev's refusal to discuss the question in the E.A.C. and, still more significant, the Soviet proposals for control machinery for Germany to cover the first period of occupation. These proposals not only advocate the use of the German central government and the German central organs for the purpose of carrying out the terms of surrender, but set out as one of the most important objectives of the Allied control agencies "the preparation of conditions for the creation in Germany of *central* and local organs based on democratic principles". It is difficult to believe that such realists as the Russians would wish to create central organs based on any principles if their purpose was to destroy the unity of Germany. At any rate we cannot take it for granted that the Soviet Government are now in favour of dismemberment.

34. Should however we find them pressing for it, we shall be faced with a dilemma. If, on the basis of the arguments in this paper, we hold out against it, the Russians may suspect our motives and regard us either as appeasers or more probably as harbouring some deep-laid plot to bring Germany one day into an anti-Soviet bloc. This would be liable to vitiate all prospect of fruitful collaboration with the Soviet Union. The Russians' reaction would probably be to adopt whatever measures they considered necessary to achieve their own security, including all kinds of intrigue and intervention in every country of Europe and possibly an attempt to collaborate closely with Germany herself in order to counteract our supposed policy. If, on the other hand, we agree to dismemberment, acute differences are almost bound to arise in course of time over its policing for the reasons given in paragraph 27. It is not impossible too that dismemberment would lead to the division of former Germany into Eastern and Western spheres of influence which it is our policy to avoid.

35. Either course, therefore, has its dangers. But the greater danger seems to lie in supporting a policy against our better judgment only to find when it had to be enforced that public support for the ruthless measures required was not forthcoming. If therefore we find the Russians bent on dismemberment but decide that such a policy would be mistaken, it would seem best to make our views and our reasons abundantly clear to them, leaving no doubt in their minds that a soft peace is no part of our plan.

36. If we can convince the Russians that we harbour no designs of using the Germans against them—a point of particular current importance in the light of the Chiefs of Staff's Report—there is no reason to believe that the

preservation of a united Germany would necessarily lead to a Russo-German combination. The more likely result of leaving Germany united would surely be to make the Russians more inclined to collaborate with us, always provided we remain strong and an Ally worth having. One can go further and suggest that the existence of a united Germany might prove a factor of the first importance in holding the Soviet Union and ourselves together.

21

Morgenthau on a Churchill-Roosevelt Agreement

Unhappy with Lord Cherwell's suggested memorandum expressing a Churchill-Roosevelt agreement on policy for postwar Germany, Morgenthau dictated his own. Although the memo dealt with only a small portion of the Morgenthau Plan, it did cover two critical issues: the punishment/reform of turning Germany into an agricultural state, and the limiting of reparations to the dismantling of German industry. The question of partition was only partially answered by the reference to the internationalization of the Saar and the Ruhr. Churchill's changes strenghtened the memo, as can be seen by comparing it with Document 1.

Document†

At a conference between the President and the Prime Minister, Mr. Churchill said that he would sum up the discussion that we had been having in regard to the future disposition of the Ruhr and the Saar. He said that they would permit Russia and any other of our Allies to help themselves to whatever machinery they wished, that the industries in the Ruhr and in the Saar would be shut down, and that these two districts would be put under an international body which would supervise these industries to see that they would not start up again.

This programme for eliminating the war-making industries in the Ruhr and in the Saar is part of a programme looking forward to diverting Germany into largely an agricultural country.

The Prime Minister and the President were in agreement upon this programme.

†From: Morgenthau, Memorandum, September 15, 1944, in U.S., Department of State, *FRUS, Quebec, 1944*, p. 390.

22

British Opposition to the Plan

At the instigation of Foreign Minister Eden, the British War Cabinet sent a message to Churchill during the Quebec Conference in which they recommended that the prime minister not commit himself or the government to the Morgenthau Plan. The basic argument was an appeal to practicality. The message argued that the policy of creating chaos simply would not work. In addition, it expressed concern at the lack of reparations and the possibility of having to provide relief for Germans who could no longer support themselves. Although the cable was based upon an inadequate understanding of the Morgenthau Plan, irreconcilable differences obviously existed between the Treasury Department plan and basic thinking within the War Cabinet. Given Churchill's reluctance (and even inability) to go directly against war cabinet decisions, this message augered a quick end of the prime minister's support for the Morgenthau Plan.

Document†

Following for Foreign Secretary.

1. As a result of Cabinet Meeting on 11th Sept. following message for you to send to Prime Minister was agreed with Deputy Prime Minister, Chancellor of Exohequer, Secretary of State for War, Minister of Production and Vice Chiefs of Staff:

"There is some evidence that the President has been converted to a policy of letting Germany stew in her own juice after the surrender, imposing or making the Germans impose few controls in the sphere of civil administration and letting chaos have its way. Those who support this policy tend to regard it as the true "hard" policy, and think it soft to try to re-establish order.

"This is a matter of great importance, since what we do or fail to do in the first few weeks will influence all that follows. A failure to maintain economic controls will lead to hoarding and eventually to another inflation, such as Germany had before.

"This would be wholly against our interests:

(A) The task of our occupation forces would be made more difficult and we should need increased forces, control personnel and administrative services (especially transportation services);

---

†From: British War Cabinet to Eden, September 14, 1944, Prime Minister's Operational Files (PREMIER 3), file 192/folder 1, pp. 8-9, Public Records Office.

(B) A few profiteers would again; the true sufferers would be the workers and the middle classes;

(C) Our name would be associated with avoidable and purposeless suffering, not with just retribution;

(D) All hopes would vanish of getting any adequate contribution out of Germany towards the reconstruction of Europe. We should be strongly pressed to send relief goods in, if only at the insistance of our own forces who would inevitably be affected by the sight of starving children.

"A policy which condenses or favours chaos is not hard; it is simply inefficient, we do not favour a soft policy towards Germany; but the suffering which she must underto should be the price of useful results for the United Nations, ordered and controlled by ourselves.

"If the President takes this line—which is contrary to everything in the plans we and the Americans have prepared—you will perhaps think fit to persuade him of its unwisdom."

2. Minister of Labour is not prepared to commit himself to views expressed in this message without more knowledge of President's proposals and fuller examination of arguments for and against them.

3. The purpose of the Message was of course to prevent a snap decision being taken on a matter which everyone agreed demands very full and careful study.

23

"The Point of Difference... is One of Means"

In a shrewdly conceived memorandum, Stimson attacked the economic proposals of the Morgenthau Plan as both impractical and un-American. Aware that the Treasury Department argued that opponents of the plan were soft on Germany, the secretary of war supported punishment of German war criminals and stern measures to prevent a redevelopment of the German military. Calling Morgenthau's proposals a "revolution," Stimson claimed that they would not work and would be interpreted as mere vengence. Paraphrasing the Atlantic Charter, the secretary argued that such treatment violated America's own principles. Stimson's vacillation between simplistic power politics (e.g., his recommendations for a military reaction to Japanese expansion prior to Pearl Harbor) and this type of appeal to moral principle make him appear inconsistent, but his feelings were obviously genuine.

Document†

Washington, September 15, 1944.

Memorandum for the President

Since the meeting with you on September 9th attended by the Secretary of State, the Secretary of the Treasury, Mr. Hopkins, and myself, I have had an opportunity to read the latest papers submitted to you by the Secretary of the Treasury on the treatment of Germany. There is no need to make any extended or detailed reply to these papers. My views have already been submitted to you in other memoranda. I merely wish to reiterate briefly that I still feel that the course proposed by the Treasury would in the long run certainly defeat what we hope to attain by a complete military victory,—this is, the peace of the world, and the assurance of social, economic and political stability in the world.

The point of difference is not one of objective,—continued world peace—it is one of means. When we discuss means, the difference is not whether we should be soft or tough on the German people; but rather whether the course proposed will in fact best attain our agreed objective, continued peace.

---

†From: Memorandum from Stimson to Roosevelt, September 15, 1944, in U.S., Department of State, *FRUS, Quebec, 1944*, pp. 482-85.

If I thought that the Treasury proposals would accomplish that objective, I would not persist in my objections. But I cannot believe that they will make a lasting peace. In spirit and in emphasis they are punitive, not, in my judgment, corrective or constructive. They will tend through bitterness and suffering to breed another war, not to make another war undesired by the Germans nor impossible in fact. It is not within the realm of possibility that a whole nation of seventy million people, who have been outstanding for many years in the arts and the sciences and who through their efficiency and energy have attained one of the highest industrial levels in Europe, can by force be required to abandon all their previous methods of life, be reduced to a peasant level with virtually complete control of industry and science left to other peoples.

The question is not whether we want Germans to suffer for their sins. Many of us would like to see them suffer the tortures they have inflicted on others. The only question is whether over the years a group of seventy million educated, and efficient and imaginative people can be kept within bounds on such a low level of subsistence as the Treasury proposals contemplate. I do not believe that is humanly possible. A subordinate question is whether even if you could do this it is good for the rest of the world either economically or spiritually. Sound thinking teaches that prosperity in one part of the world helps to create prosperity in other parts of the world. It also teaches that poverty in one part of the world usually induces poverty in other parts. Enforced poverty is even worse, for it destroys the spirit not only of the victim but debases the victor. It would be just such a crime as the Germans themselves hoped to perpetrate upon their victims—it would be a crime against civilization itself.

This country since its very beginning has maintained the fundamental belief that all men, in the long run, have the right to be free human beings and to live in the pursuit of happiness. Under the Atlantic Charter victors and vanquished alike are entitled to freedom from economic want. But the proposed treatment of Germany would, if successful, deliberately deprive many millions of people of the right to freedom from want and freedom from fear. Other peoples all over the world would suspect the validity of our spiritual tenets and question the long range effectiveness of our economic and political principles as applied to the vanquished.

The proposals would mean a forcible revolution in all of the basic methods of life of a vast section of the population as well as a disruption of many accustomed geographical associations and communications. Such an operation would naturally and necessarily involve a chaotic upheaval in the people's lives which would inevitably be productive of the deepest resentment and bitterness towards the authorities which had imposed such revolutionary changes upon them. Physically, considering the fact that their present enlarged population has been developed and supported under an entirely different geography and economy, it would doubtless cause tremendous suffering involving virtual starvation and death for many, and migrations and changes for others. It would be very difficult, if not impossible, for them to understand any purpose or cause for such revolutionary changes other than mere vengeance of their enemies and this alone would strongly tend towards the most bitter reactions.

I am prepared to accede to the argument that even if German resources were wiped off the map, the European economy would somehow readjust itself, perhaps with the help of Great Britain and this country. And the world would go on. The benefit to England by the suppression of German competition is greatly stressed in the Treasury memorandum. But this is an argument addressed to a shortsighted cupidity of the victors and the negation of all that Secretary Hull has been trying to accomplish since 1933. I am aware of England's need, but I do not and cannot believe that she wishes this kind of remedy. I feel certain that in her own interest she could not afford to follow this path. The total elimination of a competitor (who is always also a potential purchaser) is rarely a satisfactory solution of a commercial problem.

The sum total of the drastic political and economic steps proposed by the Treasury is an open confession of the bankruptcy of hope for a reasonable economic and political settlement of the causes of war.

I plead for no "soft" treatment of Germany. I urge only that we take steps which in the light of history are reasonably adapted to our purpose, namely, the prevention of future wars. The Carthaginian aspect of the proposed plan would, in my judgment, provoke a reaction on the part of the people in this country and in the rest of the world which would operate not only against the measures advocated but in its violence would sweep away the proper and reasonable restrictive measures that we could justifiably impose.

I have already indicated in my memorandum of September 9, 1944, the lines along which I would recommend that we should go pending further light on other questions which can only be obtained after we have acquired greater knowledge of conditions and trends within Germany as well as of the views and intentions of our Allies.

Henry L. Stimson
Secretary of War

24

Persuading the President Against the Plan

On the surface, the State Department position on Germany reflected in this memorandum appeared compatible with the Morgenthau Plan. Actually, it proceeded from a radically different view of the causes of World War II in Europe. The Treasury Department blamed the war purely and simply on German immorality and militarism; the State Department, while critical of Germany's overeagerness to resort to military solutions and while condemning Naziism, found the basic cause of the war in autarky—the tendency of governments to pursue narrowly nationalistic and illiberal international trade policies. Aware of Morgenthau's success in promoting his plan, this memo attempted to undermine the support given the treasury by Roosevelt.

Document†

Washington, September 29, 1944.

Memorandum for the President

The Cabinet Committee has not been able to agree upon a statement of American policy for the post-war treatment of Germany. The memorandum presented by the Secretary of the Treasury is decidedly at variance with the views developed in the State Department. In the meantime, I have received your memorandum of September 15, with the statements of views respecting the Ruhr, Saar, etc., and the conversion of Germany into an agricultural and pastoral country, which was formulated at Quebec. This memorandum seems to reflect largely the opinions of the Secretary of the Treasury in the treatment to be accorded Germany. I feel that I should therefore submit to you the line of thought that has been developing in the State Department on this matter.

1. *Status of Negotiations With the British and Russians*

The instrument of unconditional surrender of Germany has been recommended by the European Advisory Commission and has been formally approved by this Government. It is anticipated that British and Russian

†From: Memorandum from Hull to Roosevelt, September 29, 1944, in U.S., Department of State, *FRUS, Conferences at Malta and Yalta, 1945*, (Washington, D.C.: Government Printing Office, 1955), pp. 156-58.

approval will be forthcoming. The question of the American and British zones of occupation was, according to your memorandum, worked out at Quebec and there will presumably be no more difficulty over this matter. In the meantime, the European Advisory Commission is going ahead on plans for a tripartite control machinery and military government for Germany during the occupation period. All three governments have submitted proposals which are similar in their general outline. The American proposal contemplates a Supreme Authority consisting of the three Commanding Generals of the U.S., the U.K. and the U.S.S.R., which would coordinate Allied control of Germany and supervise such centralized governmental functions and economic activities as the three powers deem essential. A Control Council, composed of representatives in equal numbers from each of the three Allied Governments, would be established by the Supreme Allied Authority and will coordinate the administration of military government throughout Germany, including detailed planning for the execution of directives received from the three governments. We expect to have a recommended plan on this from the European Advisory Commission in the near future.

2. *Important Problems For Which High Policy Decisions Might Be Worked Out by the Three Governments*

The fundamental question to be decided is what kind of a Germany we want and what policy should be put into effect during occupation to attain our objectives. The most important of these problems are set forth below with an explanation of the State Department's views. It should be emphasized, however, that these objectives will have to be worked out with our principal Allies if they are to be applied throughout the German Reich.

(a) Demilitarization of Germany. The complete dissolution of all German armed forces and all Nazi military, para-military and police organizations, and the destruction or scrapping of all arms, ammunition and implements of war should be effected. Further manufacture in Germany of arms, ammunition and implements of war should be prohibited.

(b) Dissolution of the Nazi party and all affiliated organizations. The Nazi Party should be immediately dissolved. Large groups of particularly objectionable elements, especially the SS and the Gestapo, should be tried and, if found guilty, executed. Active party members should be excluded from political or civil activity and subject to a number of restrictions. All laws discriminating against persons on grounds of race, color, creed or political opinion should be annulled.

(c) Extensive controls should be maintained over communications, press and propaganda for the purpose of eliminating doctrines or similar teachings.

(d) Extensive controls over German educational system should be established for the purpose of eliminating all Nazi influence and propaganda.

(e) No decision should be taken on the possible partition of Germany (as distinguished from territorial amputations) until we see what the internal situation is and what is the attitude of our principal Allies on this question. We should encourage a decentralization of the German governmental structure and if any tendencies toward spontaneous partition of Germany arise they should not be discouraged.

(f) Economic Objectives. The primary and continuing objectives of our economic policy are: (1) to render Germany incapable of waging war, and (2) to eliminate permanently German economic domination of Europe. A shorter term objective is to require the performance by Germany of acts of restitution and reparation for injuries done to the United Nations.

To achieve the first two objectives, it will be essential (1) to destroy all factories incapable of conversion to peaceful purposes and to prevent their reconstruction, (2) to enforce the conversion of all other plants, (3) to eliminate self-sufficiency by imposing reforms that will make Germany dependent upon world markets, (4) to establish controls over foreign trade and key industries for the purpose of preventing German rearmament, and (5) to eliminate the position of power of large industrialists and land-owners.

This Government has little direct interest in obtaining reparations from Germany and no interest in building up German economy in order to collect continuing reparations. However, the U.S.S.R. and a number of other states which have been victims of German destruction and exploitation may press claims for German production and labor service for rehabilitation and construction.

Extensive controls over industry and foreign trade will be essential during the immediate period of demilitarization and dismantlement, as well as during the period of reparations. After this phase, a system of control and supervision of German industry and trade will have to be worked out in the light of world security developments. This system should be of such a character that the victor powers will be able and willing to enforce it over a considerable period.

It is of the highest importance that the standard of living of the German people in the early years be such as to bring home to them that they have lost the war and to impress on them that they must abandon all their pretentious theories that they are a superior race created to govern the world. Through lack of luxuries we may teach them that war does not pay.

25

The President's Response

Caught in a cabinet and bureaucratic hassle, Roosevelt responded in typical fashion by postponing any decision. Always convinced that problems usually resolved themselves if given enough time, the president also refused to permit the European Advisory Commission to make any sort of decisions. His long-standing agreement with Hull's liberal internationalism in trade and economics made Roosevelt agree with some of the broad principles outlined in Hull's memo of September 29 (see Document 24), but Roosevelt carefully avoided any direct repudiation of the Morgenthau Plan.

Document†

Washington, October 20, 1944.

Memorandum for the Secretary of State

In regard to your memorandum of September twenty-ninth, I think it is all very well for us to make all kinds of preparations for the treatment of Germany but there are some matters in regard to such treatment that lead me to believe that speed on these matters is not an essential at the present moment. It may be in a week, or it may be in a month, or it may be several months hence. I dislike making detailed plans for a country which we do not yet occupy.

Your memorandum paragraph No. 1

I agree except for going into too much detail and directives at the present moment, and we must emphasize the fact that the European Advisory Commission is "Advisory" and that you and I are not bound by this advice. This is something which is sometimes overlooked and if we do not remember that word "advisory" they may go ahead and execute some of the advice, which, when the time comes, we may not like at all.

Your memorandum paragraph No. 2

In view of the fact that we have not occupied Germany, I cannot agree at this moment as to what kind of a Germany we want in every detail.

In regard to the problems involved, there are some which are perfectly clear and which can be approved now.

Sub-paragraph (*a*) on the Demilitarization of Germany is, of course, correct but should include everything to do with aircraft. This should be made specific. It must apply not merely to the assembly of aircraft but to

†From: Memorandum from Roosevelt to Hull, October 20, 1944, in U.S., Department of State, *FRUS, Yalta*, pp. 158-59.

everything that goes into an aircraft. We must remember that somebody may claim that the aircraft is for non-military purposes, such as a transport plane. Germany must be prevented from making any aircraft of any type in the future.

I am in hearty agreement with Sub-paragraph (b) Dissolution of the Nazi Party and all affiliated organizations.

In the same way, I agree with Sub-Paragraph (c) Extensive controls should be maintained over communications, press and propaganda.

Sub-paragraph (d) Extensive controls over German educational system. I should like to talk with your experts in regard to just what this means.

I agree with Sub-paragraph (e) No decision should be taken on the possible partition of Germany.

Sub-paragraph (f) Economic Objectives. I should like to discuss this with the State Department in regard to some of the language. I agree with it in principle, but I do not know what part of it means. Much of this sub-head is dependent on what we and the Allies find when we get into Germany—and we are not there yet.

F[ranklin] D. R[oosevelt]

26

A Directive for Military Government in Germany: Compromise Against the Plan

Basic guidance for the American army's occupation of Germany came from this document, abbreviated as JCS 1067. Although it went through a number of revisions, its thrust remained the same. Reflecting a number of compromises between the War and Treasury departments, JCS 1067 provided extensive autonomy for the military commander while simultaneously preventing the military from rehabilitating the German economy. Treasury officials who had hoped to leave the Germans completely to their own devices, opposed the section which gave the military control over the economy, but with Roosevelt backing away from the Morgenthau Plan they had to settle for this compromise. Eventually, as Morgenthau and his staff had feared, the wide grant of authority to the military governor was used to establish a program aimed at restoring the German economy.

Document†

[Washington,] September 22, 1944.

Directive to SCAEF Regarding the Military Government of Germany in the Period Immediately Following the Cessation of Organized Resistance (Post-Defeat)

1. In the event that Rankin "C"conditions obtain in Germany or that the German forces are either defeated or surrender before you have received a directive containing policies agreed upon by the three governments of the U.S., U.K., and U.S.S.R., you will be guided by the following policies, principles and instructions.

†From: "Directive to SCAEF Regarding the Military Government of Germany in the Period Immediately Following the Cessation of Organized Resistance (Post-Defeat)" September 22, 1944, in U.S., Department of State, *FRUS, YALTA*, pp. 143-46, 152-54.

2. Prior to the defeat or surrender of Germany the primary objective of your civil affairs administration has been to aid and support your military objective: the prompt defeat of the enemy. Your objective now is primarily the occupation and administration of a conquered country with such military operations as are necessary for the complete elimination of all resistance.

3. Pending the receipt of directives containing long range policies, your objectives must be of short term and military character, in order not to prejudice whatever ultimate policies may be later determined upon. Germany will not be occupied for the purpose of liberation but as a defeated enemy nation. The clear fact of German military defeat and the inevitable consequences of aggression must be appreciated by all levels of the German population. The German people must be made to understand that all necessary steps will be taken to guarantee against a third attempt by them to conquer the world. Your aim is not oppression, but to prevent Germany from ever again becoming a threat to the peace of the world. In the accomplishment of this objective the elimination of Nazism and militarism in any of their forms and the immediate apprehension of war criminals for punishment are essential steps.

4. Your occupation and administration will be just but firm and distant. You will strongly discourage fraternization between Allied troops and the German officials and population.

5. You will establish military government over all parts of Germany under your command. Your rights, powers and status in Germany are based upon the unconditional surrender or the complete defeat of Germany.

6. *a.* By virtue of your position you are clothed with supreme legislative, executive and judicial authority in the areas occupied by forces under your command. This authority will be broadly construed and includes authority to take all measures deemed by you necessary, desirable or appropriate in relation to military exigencies and the objectives a firm military government.

b. You are authorized at your discretion to delegate the authority herein granted to you in whole or in part to members of your command and further to authorize them at their discretion to make appropriate sub-delegations.

c. You should take the necessary measures to enforce the terms of surrender and complete the disarmament of Germany.

d. The Military Government shall be a military administration which, until you receive further advices, will show the characteristics of an Allied undertaking acting in the interests of the United Nations.

7. The administrative policies shall be uniform throughout those parts of Germany occupied by forces under your command subject to any special requirements due to local circumstances.

8. Representatives of civilian agencies of the U.S., U.K. and U.S.S.R. governments shall not participate unless and until you consider such participation desirable. Representatives of the civilian agencies of other Allied Governments or of UNRRA may participate only upon your recommendation and the approval of the Combined Chiefs of Staff.

9. It is contemplated that a tripartite administration by the U.S., U.K. and U.S.S.R., covering the whole of Germany will be established. You have previously received advices in this connection.

10. You are authorized as SCAEF to enter into arrangements with the U.S.S.R. military commanders as may be necessary for the occupation of Germany by the three powers.

11. Military administration shall be directed toward the promotion of the decentralization of the political structure of Germany. In the administration of areas under your command, all dealings in so far as possible should be with municipal and provincial government officials rather than with Central government officials. . . .

Appendix "A"
Political Directive

1. You will search out, arrest, and hold, pending receipt by you of further instructions as to their disposition, Adolf Hitler, his chief Nazi associates, all persons suspected of having committed war crimes, and all persons who, if permitted to remain at large, would endanger the accomplishment of your objectives. The following is a list of the categories of persons to be arrested in order to carry out this policy. If after you have entered the country and in the light of conditions which you encounter there you do not believe all of these persons should be subjected immediately to this treatment, you should report back giving your recommendations and the reasons therefor.

(a) Officials of the Nazi party and of units or branches of the Nazi party, down to and including the leaders of local party units, as well as officials of equivalent stature in associations affiliated with the Nazi party;

(b) All political police, including the Gestapo and Sicherheitsdienst der S.S.;

(c) The officers and non-commissioned officers of the Waffen S.S. and all members of the other branches of the S.S.

(d) All high officials of the police and of the SA;

(e) The leading officials of all ministries and other high political officials of Germany and those persons who have held high positions, either civil or military, in the administration of German occupied countries;

(f) Nazis and Nazi sympathizers holding important and key positions in (1) National and Gau civic and economic organizations; (2) corporations and other organizations in which the government has a major financial interest; (3) industry; (4) finance; (5) education; (6) judiciary; (7) the press, publishing houses and other agencies disseminating news and propaganda. It may generally be assumed in the absence of evidence to the contrary that any persons holding such positions are Nazis or Nazi sympathizers;

(g) All judges, prosecutors and officials of the People's Court;

(h) Any national of any of the United Nations who is believed to have committed offenses against his national law in support of the German war effort;

(*i*) Any other person whose name or designation appears on lists to be submitted to you or whose name may be notified to you separately.

Of equal if not greater importance in the ultimate destruction of German Militarism is the elimination of the German Professional Officer Corps as an institution. All General Staff Corps officers who are not taken into custody as prisoners of war should therefore be arrested and held pending receipt of further instructions as to their disposition. You will receive further instructions as to how to deal with other members of the German Officers Corps. . . .

Appendix "C"
Economic Directive

1. You shall assume such control of existing German industrial, agricultural, utility, communication and transportation facilities, supplies, and services, as are necessary for the following purposes:

a. Assuring the immediate cessation of the production, acquisition or development of implements of war;

b. Assuring, to the extent that it is feasible, the production and maintenance of goods and services essential (1) for the prevention or alleviation of epidemic or serious disease and serious civil unrest and disorder which would endanger the occupying forces and the accomplishment of the objectives of the occupation; and (2) for the prosecution of the war against Japan (but only to the extent that specific directives of higher authority call for such goods or services).

c. Preventing the dissipation or sabotage of German resources and equipment which may be required for relief, restitution, or reparation to any of the allied countries, pending a decision by the appropriate Allied governments whether and to what extent German resources or equipment will be used for such purposes.

Except for the purposes specified above, you will take no steps looking toward the economic rehabilitation of Germany nor designed to maintain or strengthen the German economy. Except to the extent necessary to accomplish the purposes set out above, the responsibility for such economic problems as price controls, rationing, unemployment, production, reconstruction, distribution, consumption, housing or transportation will remain with the German people and the German authorities. . . .

Appendix "D"
Relief Directive

You will be responsible for the provision and distribution of supplies for civilian relief only to the extent necessary to prevent disease and such disorder as might endanger or impede military occupation. For this purpose you will make maximum use of supplies, stockpiles and resources available within Germany in order to limit the extent to which imports, if any, will be required. German import requirements shall be strictly limited to minimum quotas of critical items and shall not, in any instance, take precedence over fulfillment of the supply requirements of any liberated territory. . . .

27

Opposition to the Compromise

Aware that he had been boxed in by the Treasury and War departments' agreement on JCS 1067, Secretary of State Hull tried to leave himself some room in wich to maneuver taking exception to part of the economic directive in the interim directive sent to SCAEF. Hull's opposition was directed at the clause which prohibited any action designed to rehabilitate the German economy or industry. The exception, put in the form of a letter to Stimson, had no effect upon the authority of JCS 1067. The following excerpt is John McCloy reading to Morgenthau the text of a letter sent to Stimson by Hull.

Document†

M: Now, Mr. Hull's letter to the Secretary of War was this: he said, "I understand that representatives of the State, War and Treasury Departments have been conferring for the purpose of preparing an interim directive to Eisenhower's Headquarters in regard to the military government of Germany for the period immediately following the cessation of organized resistance, and I further understand that agreement has been reached on all points with the sole exception of the final paragraph of Section One of the Appendix, which is the economic directive. This department is prepared to agree to Section One as now drafted on the understanding that the Supreme Commander is authorized to interpret this section as enabling him to retain or impose such economic controls as he may deem essential to the safety and health of the occupying forces."

†From: Transcript of Telephone Conversation between Morgenthau and McCloy September 28, 1944, in U.S., Congress, Senate, Subcommittee to Investigate the Administration of the Internal Security Act and Other Internal Security Laws of the Committee on the Judiciary,*Morgenthau Diaries,* 90th Cong., 1st sess., 2 vols. (Washington, D.C.: Government Printing Office, 1967), vol. I, p. 659.

28

Churchill and Stalin on Germany and America, October, 1944

The British minutes of the Churchill-Stalin Meeting in Moscow in October, 1944, did not become available to the public until 1972. They contained a record which varies significantly from the description of the talks found in Churchill's memoirs. Although the prime minister makes no mention of the Morgenthau Plan after his brief recounting of the 1944 Quebec Conference, the TOLSTOY minutes show that he gave it strong support during his talks with Stalin. This conference was also the scene of the famous "percent" agreement between Stalin and Churchill, and their closing comment below indicates their paternalistic approach to European politics. Although Stalin frequently teased Churchill about being too easy on the Germans, these minutes demonstrate that the Englishman was quite willing to impose a harsh peace on Germany. Churchill's willingness to see a large number of Germans killed in action, and his suggestion that massive population transfers should take place in East Prussia and Silesia (eastern Germany) both indicate his desire to inflict punishment upon the Germans.

Document†

THE PRIME MINISTER suggested that in the presence of Mr. Harriman they might have a talk about the future of Germany. He suggested that for about a month or so they should not say anything publicly because it would make the Germans fight harder. He had been shy of breathing fire and slaughter, but they might discuss it quietly among themselves.

MARSHAL STALIN agreed.

THE PRIME MINISTER said he was all for hard terms. Opinions were divided in the United States. The best thing would be to beat the Germans into unconditional surrender and then tell them what to do. He wanted to hear Marshal Stalin's opinion about the régime to be applied and how Germany was to be divided, what was to be done with Prussia, the Saar and the Ruhr, and with German weapons. Russian factories had been destroyed as

†From: Records of the Meetings at the Kremlin, Moscow, October 9-17, 1944 (TOLSTOY), Prime Minister's Operational Files, PREM 3/434/2/61-62, 92-94, pp. 8-9, Public Records Office.

well as Belgian and Dutch and the machines taken away would have to be replaced. Perhaps the Foreign Secretaries could discuss this matter with M. Molotov and Mr. Harriman.

The President was for hard terms. Others were for soft. The problem was how to prevent Germany getting on her feet in the lifetime of grandchildren.

MARSHAL STALIN thought the Versailles peace was inadequate. It had not removed the possibility of revenge. Hard measures would stir a desire for revenge. The problem was to create such a peace that the possibility of revenge would be denied to Germany. Her heavy industry would have to be destroyed. The State would have to be split up. How that was to be done would have to be discussed. Her heavy industry would have to be reduced to a minimum.

THE PRIME MINISTER suggested it should apply to the electrical and chemical industries also.

MARSHAL STALIN agreed that it should apply to all industry producing war material. Germany should be deprived of the possibility of revenge. Otherwise every twenty-five or thirty years there would be a new world war which would exterminate the young generation. If approached from that angle the harshest measures would prove to be the most humane. Eight to ten million Germans had been lost after every war. Reprisals in Germany might not affect only one and a half million Germans. As regards concrete proposals, Mr. Eden and M. Molotov should get together.

M. MOLOTOV asked what was the Prime Minister's opinion of the Morgenthau plan.

THE PRIME MINISTER said that the President and Mr. Morgenthau were not very happy about its reception. The Prime Minister went on to say that as he had declared in Tehran, Britain would not agree to mass execution of Germans, because one day British public opinion would cry out. But it was necessary to kill as many as possible in the field. The others should be made to work to repair the damage done to other countries. They might use the Gestapo on such work and the Hitler Youth should be re-educated to learn that it was more difficult to build than to destroy.

MARSHAL STALIN thought that a long occupation of Germany would be necessary.

THE PRIME MINISTER did not think that the Americans would stay very long.

MARSHAL STALIN said France should provide some forces.

THE PRIME MINISTER agreed.

MARSHAL STALIN suggested the use of the small countries.

THE PRIME MINISTER thought United Poland could be employed.

MARSHAL STALIN said Silesia would go to the Poles and part of East Prussia. The Soviet Union would take Koenigsberg and the Poles would be very interested in the occupation of Germany.

THE PRIME MINISTER thought the population might be moved from Silesia and East Prussia to Germany. If seven million had been killed in the war there would be plenty of room for them. He suggested that M. Molotov and Mr. Eden, with Mr. Harriman, should talk this over and get a picture of the general proposals for Marshal Stalin and himself to think about, and thus when the end came they would not be without something unprobed. They should also decide what part the European Advisory Commission should play.

MARSHAL STALIN agreed. . . .

Dismemberment of Germany

MARSHAL STALIN asked what they were to do with Germany.

THE PRIME MINISTER asked Mr. Eden to make his suggestions.

MR. EDEN explained that we had come to no conclusion but there were three alternative courses:—

(1) Dismemberment, without any relation to the old German States
(2) To use some of the old States as a basis.
(3) To impose a permanent international control on the chief industrial area, the Rhine, the Ruhr, the Saar and Westfalia, after Russia and the other Allies had taken what they needed in material. This area would be separated from Germany.

MARSHAL STALIN asked: Who would exercise control over the industrial area?

MR. EDEN replied: The Allies.

MARSHALL STALIN asked if it would only be economic control.

MR. EDEN replied that it would be a general control.

THE PRIME MINISTER thought that Prussia was the root of the evil and the Prussian military caste.

MARSHAL STALIN said that Prussia contributed the man-power.

THE PRIME MINISTER suggested the isolation of Prussia and control over the Ruhr and the Saar. How this was to be done could be discussed later. First, it was necessary to take away all the machinery and machine tools that Russia, Belgium, Holland and France needed. He would support Marshal Stalin in repairing the damage to Russia's Western provinces which had suffered so much. It was only fair. The same applied to the smaller Allies. This was the policy which Mr. Morgenthau had laid before the President—to put the Ruhr and Saar out of action. Mr. Morgenthau's hatred of the Germans was indescribable.

MARSHAL STALIN said he must be a second Vansittart.

THE PRIME MINISTER said that the President had liked what Morgenthau had said.

Continuing, he asked why the British should not make the things needed by Europe fair competiton with other countries. After this war Britain would be the only great debtor nation. Their foreign securities, amounting to £400,000,000 had been sold. Britain's sterling debts now amounted to £3,000 million. She would have to make every effort to increase her exports to buy food. Russia's intention to take away German machinery was in harmony with Britain's interests of filling in the gap in the place of Germany. This was only justice.

MARSHAL STALIN said he would support any steps taken by Britain to receive compensation for the losses she had suffered.

THE PRIME MINISTER said he would support Russia in getting the machine tools required by the Ukraine and other ravaged regions.

The Prime Minister went on to say that they had not been thinking of Germany up to that point. They must now devote their minds to that problem. He would not trust Germany with the development of her metallurgy, chemical or electrical industries. He would stop those altogether for as long as he had a word to say, and he hoped for a generation at least. He had not thought about the division of Prussia, but only of its isolation and of cutting off those two centres, the Ruhr and the Saar, from Prussia. They were centres of war production and machine building.

MARSHAL STALIN asked if he was to understand that Mr. Churchill's suggestion provided for an independent State of Prussia after the cession of territory to Poland.

THE PRIME MINISTER replied that Poland would get a slice of East Prussia and Silesia. The Kiel Canal would be neutralised. The Ruhr and the Saar would be put permanently out of action.

MARSHAL STALIN asked whether the Ruhr and the Saar would be separate States.

THE PRIME MINISTER said that he had only been thinking of destroying industry. He had a vivid memory of the last war. We had stopped Germany from having an army, navy and air force. We had destroyed her weapons.

MARSHAL STALIN interrupted to say that it was unwise to destory Germany's weapons. The navy should not be sunk and artillery should not be blown up. They might be useful against Japan.

THE PRIME MINISTER suggested that Russia could take what she wanted.

MARSHAL STALIN thought Britain could use some of Germany's ships.

THE PRIME MINISTER replied that Russia could do the same, but in the future air would be stronger than the fleet.

MARSHAL STALIN said that Great Powers could not be without navies. Germany's mistake was that she had wanted to conquer Europe although she had no fleet. The point was she had no fuel in Europe and was short of food, and a fleet was necessary to carry fuel and food. Germany had not understood this.

THE PRIME MINISTER said that Britain intended to maintain a strong fleet and a strong air component. She would welcome the appearance of a strong Russian fleet on all the seas. She would create no obstacles to Russia's having a fleet.

THE PRIME MINISTER went on to say that after the last war Rathenau had told the Germans after they had been deprived of their army and navy that it would not matter. He would arrange factories and make new weapons. If factories were arranged Germany would become a great Power quicker than any of the others. Brüning carried on with this policy, but no one dared go into production until Hitler appeared. Hitler did not invent this theme.

Rathenau and Brüning had thought of it. Hitler only pulled the lever. It should not happen again. Industrial disarmament was the important thing. To begin with, the machine tools must be taken away.

MARSHAL STALIN agreed and added that all metallurgical works should be destroyed. They were difficult to restore. Germany produced four times more pig iron than England.

A map of Germany was then produced.

Marshal Stalin asked whether France wanted access to the Rhine.

THE PRIME MINISTER said that France wanted the West bank of the Rhine internationalised. Czechoslovakia was ready to give up a small area near Eger, but wanted some readjustment of the frontier in the North for strategic reasons.

The Prime Minister suggested that Bavaria and Austria should go together with Vienna as the capital and form a separate State with Würtemberg and Baden. There would be three States in Germany: Bavaria and Austria—soft treatment. Prussia—hard treatment. The industrial area on the Rhine—under international control. Saxony, when stripped, might go to Prussia.

MR. EDEN pointed out that if in the future Bavaria again wanted to combine with Prussia she might draw Austria after her.

MARSHAL STALIN said that Hungary would have to remain a separate State. Neither the Hungarians nor the Slavs should ever form part of any German State. They were too weak and Germany was too cultured. Germany would quickly dominate them. Marshal Stalin said that the small nations in Europe should be made to police Germany. The Poles would be glad to take a hand in the occupation. The Poles deserved to get territory on their Western borders. They had suffered much for over a century.

THE PRIME MINISTER asked what the Marshal thought of Poland, Czechoslovakia and Hungary forming a separate grouping.

MARSHAL STALIN asked whether it would be an *entente*.

THE PRIME MINISTER explained that it would be more than an *entente*, it would be a Zollverein. The evil in Europe was that travelling across it one used many different currencies, passed a dozen frontiers, many customs barriers, and all this was a great obstacle to trade. He wanted to see Europe prosperous and some of the old glory return to her. In this way perhaps hatred would die. He thought this might be achieved by groupings for commercial and trade purposes.

MARSHAL STALIN suggested that this question might crop up somewhat later but the immediate point was that after this war all States would be very nationalistic. The Hungarians, Czechs and Poles would first want to build up their national life and not restrict their own rights by combining with others. The feeling to live independently would be the strongest. Later, economic feelings would prevail, but in the first period they would be purely nationalistic and therefore groupings would be unwelcome. The fact that Hitler's regime had developed nationalism could be seen in the example of Yugoslavia where Croats. Montenegrius, Slovenes, &c., all wanted something of their own. It was a symptom.

M. MOLOTOV said that after the last war many new small States had been formed. Many of them had failed. It would be dangerous to go to the other extreme after this war and to force States to form groups. It would be impossible for Czechs and Hungarians to unite and to find a common language immediately after this war. Nor could the Czechs and Poles do so. They all had a great desire for an independent life. The fact was that their independence had been of short duration.

THE PRIME MINISTER hoped that some of the young men present would see it.

MARSHAL STALIN thought that Mr. Churchill's suggestion would be possible in the future but not just yet.

THE PRIME MINISTER suggested that Germany should be deprived of all her aviation.

MARSHAL STALIN agreed and suggested that neither civil nor military flying should be allowed. All training schools for pilots should be forbidden.

THE PRIME MINISTER said that Mr. Morgenthau had suggested that Germany should have no merchant shipping. She should be made to hire ships from other countries to carry her goods.

MARSHAL STALIN agreed and said that a merchant fleet provided manpower for the navy. The absence of a merchant fleet prevented the creation of a navy.

THE PRIME MINISTER thought that there was very little divergence of opinion between them. It was a pity that when God created the world he had not consulted them.

MARSHAL STALIN said it was God's first mistake.

MR. EDEN suggested that M. Gusev should get on with the preparatory work in the E.A.C.

MARSHAL STALIN said that the principles should be laid down by the three governments and that the E.A.C. should be given some guidance. . . .

29

British Arguments Against the Plan

By December, 1944, the British Foreign Office had developed a full set of arguments against the Morgenthau Plan's proposal for the deindustrialization of the Ruhr and Saar areas. Countering arguments that deindustrialization would benefit British trade, the Foreign Office sounded remarkably like Cordell Hull and the State Department when it claimed that Germany played an integral role in the entire structure of the world economy.

Document†

14. Our conclusions may be summarised as follows:—

(a) The direct and indirect effects on the Rhineland, Westphalia and the Saar of eliminating the metal, chemical and engineering industries in that area would be to deprive of their normal livelihood about 2 million of the pre-war working population of 6½ million. The short-term prospects of absorbing these unemployed in other industries in the area are bad and even on a long view the creation of new industries could never enable the area to support the high density of population which it has done in the past with a standard of living comparable with the rest of Germany. Agriculture is already carried out intensively in the area and could not absorb an appreciable amount of additional labour.

(b) The absorption of these 2 million unemployed in the rest of Germany would be very difficult if at the same time 3 to 5 million workers from the ceded territories of the East had also to be absorbed. Some 600,000 could expect to find immediate work in agriculture, and over a period of from 10 to 15 years a policy of breaking up the larger estates might result in the settling on the land of a further 720,000 if East Prussia and Silesia only are ceded or 570,000 if all the area east of the Oder is ceded. The capital investment needed for this and for the development of new industries to absorb the remainder would be very substantial, and its provision would be made even more difficult by the repercussions of the proposals on Germany's exports and her balance of trade. The industries in question normally provide some 60

†From: A.P.W. (44) 127, December 27, 1944, War Cabinet, Foreign Office 371/46720/4010, pp. 6-7, Public Records Office.

per cent of Germany's exports and the loss of production would far exceed the amounts normally exported so that a serious decline in exports could scarcely be avoided. Indeed, the change in pattern of the economy would cause acute problems of re-adjustment which might well call for additional imports during the period of changeover.

(c) Since Germany's exports might well not be sufficient even to pay for her essential imports, there might be no reparation at all apart from certain "once for all" deliveries.

(d) If the elimination of the industries concerned were permanently secured the objective of economic security would be achieved, but these proposals would be less likely to be effective than similar measures applied over the whole of Germany to selected industries covering a smaller field. Moreover, it seems doubtful whether it would be possible in practice to achieve the permanent elimination of these industries.

(e) The effects of the proposals on British commercial interests would be conflicting. The destruction would tend to improverish not only Germany but the world as a whole. On the other hand, in so far as the industries concerned are competitive with our own, we could hope to obtain a share of their former markets which would considerably exceed our pre-war share of German imports, and should be larger than any loss we might sustain in other exports through the increased competition from permitted German industries. Of the latter, coal is the most important. The loss of some of our traditional markets to Germany would reduce any net gain in visible trade to a figure nearer £300 to £400 million which has been suggested. On invisible account our prospects of obtaining anything on account of the substantial British investments in Germany would be further reduced.

(f) The effects upon France, Belgium and Luxembourg would probably be similar to the effects on the United Kingdom. Denmark and Norway would probably be adversely affected by the loss of the German market. Although Holland might gain in the long run from expansion of her industry, she would also lose the German market for her agricultural produce and a valuable entrepot trade. S.E. Europe would be unlikely to gain anything, but should not lose in the long run since Austria, Czechoslovakia and perhaps the Soviet Union would tend to replace Germany both as a source of supply and a market.

5th December, 1944.

30

"The Department of State Believes..."

The State Department never altered its views during the entire debate over postwar planning for Germany. Hull's departure merely meant a different signature at the bottom of memoranda for Roosevelt. Invariably the arguments boiled down to two basic points; that a program of deindustrialization was impractical, and that Germany had a positive role to play in the world economy. Stettinius's strong support for a severe policy was belied by his final sentence.

Document†

[Washington,] November 22, 1944.

Subject: Summary of Department's Views on Economic Treatment of Germany

The Department of State believes:

(1) The German economy should be operated as nearly as possible *as a unit* during the occupation period.

(2) Allied occupation policy should be *severe—*

(*a*) a rock-bottom standard of living for the Germans;

(*b*) labor services for the rehabilitation of devastated parts of Europe;

(*c*) transfer of such industrial equipment and stockpiles as liberated countries can put to effective use, limited only by necessity for maintaining a minimum German economy;

(*d*) conversion of the German economy to peacetime production, including production for minimum German needs and for reconstruction of rest of Europe on reparation account;

(*e*) elimination from positions of control of those industrial and financial leaders who have been closely identified with the Nazi regime; or who have derived large benefit from Aryanization or spoilation of occupied countries.

(3) We must rely on an effective international security organization to keep Germany disarmed. We can't make Germany so weak that it will be impossible for her to recover. A look at Russia in 1920 and in 1940 demonstrates how quickly industrial strength can be built up if a country is

†From: Memorandum from Stettinius to Roosevelt, November 22, 1944, in U.S., Department of State, *FRUS, Yalta*, p. 173.

left alone "to stew in its own juice". Disarmament requires prohibitions of arms and aircraft production and destruction of specialized facilities for their manufacture. Some other permanent or semi-permanent industrial restrictions and controls may be necessary, but if the security organization is prepared to use force to prevent rearmament, we don't have to cut deep into the German economy, and if it isn't, no amount of once-and-for-all economic destruction will make much lasting difference.

(4) In the long run, we should look forward to a German economy geared into a liberal world economy on the basis of efficient specialization. This will imply quitable German access to export markets, abolition of German self-sufficiency, and abandonment of instruments of German economic aggression—private international cartels, bilateral barter arrangements, etc. This alone is compatible with the emergence of a stable non-agressive Germany. This may prove to be unattainable, but for the present we should take no action which would premanently preclude peaceful development of Germany.

E.R. Stettinius, Jr.

31

Morgenthau Defends the Plan

Shortly before Roosevelt left for the Yalta Conference, Morgenthau prepared a statement which summed up the basic concept of the program he proposed for postwar Germany. Defensive in tone, the Treasury secretary chose to send it only to the State Department instead of to the president. His reference in paragraph 1.(b) to the provocative nature of any plan to use Germany as a buffer against Russia indicated his belief that such notions had become the major reason for State Department opposition to the Morgenthau Plan.

Document†

[Washington], January 19, 1945.

Memorandum

Re: *Long Range Program for Germany*

1. The single objective of any long range program towards Germany is that of doing all that we can now to prevent Germany from starting a third World War in the next generation. To accomplish this objective, the following principles are clear:

(*a*) Germany must be rendered weak politically, militarily and economically and must be kept weak for many years to come.

(*b*) Any program which has as its purpose the building up of Germany as a bulwark against Russia and communism will inevitably lead to a third World War.

(*c*) It is impossible to devise a program for Germany today which will *guarantee* peace in the years to come. We can not expect to find a panacea. There are certain minimum steps which we must take now. Developments in the next five or ten years may require that we take additional steps at that time. So long as the German people retain the will to wage war, we must be ever vigilant to see to it that they do not obtain the means to exercise this will.

(*d*) Since the stakes are so high, our goal must be that of seeing how far we can go in making certain that Germany is unable to embark upon another war rather than trying to find a minimum program which would convince most people that we had solved the problem.

---

†From: Memorandum from Morgenthau to the President (not sent), January 19, 1945, in U.S., Department of State, *FRUS, Yalta*, pp. 175-76.

2. There are many essential facts to a long range program for Germany. Without intending at all to exclude from consideration the other essential elements of the program, it is desired at this time to emphasize the importance of dealing effectively with German heavy industry because industry represents an indispensable means by which Germany can exercise her will to wage war again. Although political, military and economic controls over Germany in the post-war period are essential, they afford no reasonable assurance that a strong industrial Germany could not within twenty to thirty years again plunge the world into war. In order to make reasonably sure that we have deprived Germany of the ability to make war again within the next generation, it is absolutely essential that she be deprived of her chemical, metallurgical and electrical industries. Although this does not mean that other measures are unnecessary, the elimination of heavy industry is one of the essential steps we must take now.

At the same time that German heavy industry is eliminated in Germany every effort should be made to build up heavy industry in the liberated countries surrounding Germany. The industrial equipment moved from Germany as well as the resources in the Rhine and Ruhr areas could make a real contribution toward such a program. In this way the whole balance of industrial power in Europe will be shifted so that Germany will no longer be the dominating power in Europe.

3. After careful study, we completely reject the following propositions:

(a) The fallacy that Europe needs a strong industrial Germany.

(b) The contention that recurring reparations (which would require immediate reconstruction of the German economy) are necessary so that Germany may be made to pay for the destruction she has caused.

(c) The belief that the removal or destruction of all German war materials and the German armament industry would in itself prevent Germany from waging another war.

(d) The illogical assumption that a "soft" peace would facilitate the growth of democracy in Germany.

(e) The fallacy that making Germany a predominantly agricultural country, with light industries but no heavy industries, would mean starving Germans.

32

An American Ambassador on the Future of Germany, February, 1945

Frustrated by his inability to obtain clear and firm policy guidance from Washington, the American ambassador in London, John Winant, gave voice to his annoyance as well as his fears of the Soviet Union in a conversation with a Treasury Department official on February 1, 1945. Winant obviously supported the overall State Department position regarding Germany.

Document†

The Ambassador then made what to me was a curious remark until he explained it. He stated that we was greatly worried by some of the thinking of the people today. It developed that the thinking that was worrying him was some of the thinking on the post-war treatment of Germany. According to the Ambassador there is going to be all sorts of misery and disorder in Germany and it will be such that it is going to create just the thing we are fighting against—another Hitler.

Not knowing exactly what the Ambassador was hinting at, I made a rather general statement that conditions there would no doubt be very bad. In view of the policy of the Nazi fanatics to resist until the last man, and apparently there would be terrible destruction in the country, but I was not quite clear how this was going to create another Hitler. The Ambassador then went into a long discourse which finally added up the fact that the thinking now is to divide Germany into zones, each of which will be controlled by the particular country occupying that zone. There will be no free intercourse between the zones. In fact, it will amount to something like independent states, each of which will be a "water-tight compartment." This was a great mistake and the responsibility for it would be ours. Many who advocate this type of thinking overlooked one thing, namely, that we were going to sign the unconditional surrender terms on behalf of certain of the other United Nations whose forces have not participated in the occupation. The British would have a good defense in that they originally had wanted to bring these other countries into

†From: James Mann, Memorandum of a Conversation with Winant, February 1, 1945, in *Morgenthau Diary, Germany*, vol. 2, pp. 947-48.

the occupation work. The Russians have sided with us, but on the other hand the Russians had wanted an overall control. The advocates of the "Separate Zones" theory also overlooked the fact that whether we had a hard peace or a soft peace we should have to have some machinery for control. The Ambassador had attempted in the European Advisory Committee to set up such a machinery. The machinery had been set up with the idea that there would be an abundance of food in one zone and a scarcity in another. The food could be shipped from the abundant zone to the scarce zone, and the same applied to coal and many other things. Railroads could run throughout Germany and there would be communications throughout Germany, but under the thinking which the Ambassador was criticizing there would be no such transportation or communications. Railroads would stop at the zone line of demarcation. Hunger in one zone could not be alleviated with food from another. Then at the only point in the conversation in which the Treasury was mentioned, he said "Some of the Treasury's fellows thinking on this problem have even gone so far as to advocate the use of different currencies in different zones." That to the Ambassador was unthinkable.

At this point the Ambassador ceased talking in terms of the different zones and talked in terms of the misery that would befall Germany and the Germans. He wanted a hard peace but the way we should have that peace was by setting up a control machinery which would force the Germans to carry out our will. There had to be a certain amount of discipline and a certain amount of order. We would have sufficient troops to run the water system, to mine the coal, to make the electric plants run. We should have the Germans do this, but the way to do it was to tell them what to do and make them do it.

According to the Ambassador, however, there are a lot of people thinking about this problem who wanted to control the other. The Ambassador certainly wanted to take the "plus" and use it to repay the countries that had been devastated, but there are certain obligations which we had to assume. We had to keep a certain amount of discipline and order. How could we benefit if Germany were swept with epidemics? He could not see how that would help us at all, and he predicted that there would be great epidemics which "would not recognize uniform or nationality." He then mentioned that one had to admire the Russians for their efficiency and for their discipline. I asked what kind of controls the Russians had indicated that they would put in their zone. He said that they would keep discipline and that they would move into the zone and carry everything away, "even the machine tools." He referred at this point to their moving into Rumania and taking the American property in the oil field. He was not critical of that action, because the Russians needed oil to keep their Army going and he certainly wanted to see those Armies go. But, after the war when the fighting was over, the question was a different one. (He was not optimistic about the future, because the Russians would move in and devastate that area and anything that was given to the other United Nations to repay them for the damage they had suffered would have to come from our zone and the British zone. He again pointed out that by signing the unconditional surrender terms on behalf of certain of the other United Nations, we assumed an obligation to them.) The Ambassador seemed to fear that not only would it create a situation out of which would arrive the very thing against which we were fighting but that we would also run the risk of offending some of the other United Nations.

During this conversation I said very little. In fact, there was not much opportunity for me to talk and when the Ambassador started explaining his point of view I was careful not to interrupt him. Most of my comments were of a very general nature and generally referred to the newspapers and points of view I had seen expressed in the British press. At the end of our interview I mentioned generally to the Ambassador that I was somewhat disturbed by some of the thinking which I had seen expressed in the British press. I mentioned that the press talked quite a bit in terms of reparation as distinguished from restitution. That meant the retention of German industry and thus meant the retention of the German war potential. The Ambassador recognized that there were some British people who felt like that but certainly not all. He said it would be unthinkable if we let the German war potential and he certainly didn't propose to do that. At this point the Ambassador stopped discussing the post-war treatment of Germany and I was unable to draw him out further on any of the topics which he had mentioned.

33

Stalin, Churchill, and Roosevelt on Reparations

The question of reparations, only partially settled at Yalta, eventually became the specific issue which brought on Soviet-American disagreement in Germany. In this discussion, the attitudes of the Big Three become very clear. The Russians were willing to permit a moderate redevelopment of German industry so that reparations could be paid; the British believed overly harsh reparations demands would embitter the Germans and eventually force the Allies to provide economic assistance to prevent starvation; and the Americans tried to split the difference.

Document†

MR. MAISKY then outlined the Soviet plan for reparations for Germany. He said that the Soviet plan for reparations in kind envisaged two categories: (1) the removal from the national wealth of Germany of plants, machine tools, rolling stock, etc. to be completed within a period of two years after the end of hostilities, (2) yearly payments in kind to last for ten years. He said that in order to restore Soviet economy which had suffered so much from German aggression, and to safeguard the future security of Europe, it would be necessary to reduce German heavy industry by 80%. By heavy industry he meant iron and steel, electrical power and chemical industries. Specialized industry useful only for military purposes should be 100% removed. In this category would fall all aviation factories, synthetic oil refineries, etc. He said that the Soviet Government felt that with 20% of her heavy industry Germany would be in position to cover the economic needs of the country. He said the list of goods to be delivered during the 10 year period could be definitely fixed later on. He further proposed that in the interests of the orderly execution of the reparations plan and for the security of Europe there should be an Anglo-Soviet-American control over German economy which would last beyond the period of the reparations payment. All German enterprises which could be utilized for war purposes should be placed under international control with representatives of the Three Powers sitting on the boards of such enterprises. Mr. Maisky went on to say that in the

†From: Bohlen Miniutes of the Second Plenary Meeting of the Crimea Conference, February 5, 1945, in U.S., Department of State, *FRUS, Yalta*, pp. 620-22.

calculation of losses as a result of German aggression the figures had been so astronomical that a selection and the establishment of a system of priorities for compensation had been necessary. He said that even direct material losses, such as public and private property, factories, plants, railroads, houses, institutions, confiscation of materials, etc. had been so large that no reparations could cover their loss. For this reason, priorities had been established according to indices, (1) the proportional contribution of any one nation to the winning of the war, (2) the material losses suffered by each nation. He said that those countries which had made the highest contribution to the war and had suffered the highest material losses would come into the first category and all others would fall into the second. Mr. Maisky proposed that there should be set up a special reparations committee of the three governments to sit in Moscow. He concluded that the total reparations shown in withdrawals and yearly payments in kind which the Soviets required would reach a total of ten billion dollars.

THE PRIME MINISTER stated that he recalled very well the end of the last war and that although he did not participate in the peace settlement he had been very fully informed of the discussions. He remembered well that there had been only two billion pounds extracted from Germany in the form of reparations by the Allies after the last war and that even this would not have been possible had not the United States given Germany credits. He said, for example, that they had taken some old Atlantic liners from the Germans, who had immediately proceeded on credit to build new and better ships. He recognized that the suffering which the Soviet Union had undergone in this war had been greater than any other power, but he felt that the Soviet Union would get nowhere near the sum which Mr. Manisky had mentioned from Germany. He said that at the end of the last war the Allies had also indulged themselves with fantastic figures of reparations but that these had turned out to be a myth. He said that the British Isles had also suffered in this war and that the British Government had disposed of the bulk of its assets abroad despite the generous help of Lend-Lease. He said that the British Isles had to export goods in order to import food, since they were dependent on imports for one-half of their food supply. He said that there would be no victorious country so burdened in an economic sense as Great Britain and that, therefore, if he could see any benefit to Great Britain in large reparations from Germany he would favor such a course but he very much doubted whether this was feasible. He added that other countries, such as Belgium, Holland and Norway also had claims against Germany. He said he was haunted by the specter of a starving Germany which would present a serious problem for the Allies since we could either say "It serves them right" or endeavor to help them. In the latter case, who would pay for the help. The Prime Minister concluded that if you wished a horse to pull a wagon that you would at least have to give it fodder.

MARSHAL STALIN observed that that was right, but care should be taken to see that the horse did not turn around and kick you.

THE PRESIDENT remarked that he had also been through the last war and that he remembered very vividly that the United States had lost a great deal of money. He said that we had lent over ten billion dollars to Germany and that this time we would not repeat our past mistakes. He said that in the United States after the last war the German property that had been sequestered during the war had been turned back to the German owners, but that this time he would seek the necessary legislation to retain for the United States all German property in America. He said that the Germans had no capital, factories, or other equipment that the United States needed but that he did not wish to have to contemplate the necessity of helping the Germans to keep from starving. He said, however, that he would willingly support any claims for Soviet reparations since he felt that the German standard of living should not be higher than that of the Soviet Union. He added that just as we expected to help Great Britain expand her export trade, we would also help the Soviet Union retain the reparations in kind which she required, as well as German manpower to reconstruct the devastated regions, but he felt that the Germans should be allowed to live in order that they might not become a burden on the world. The President concluded, however, that despite his desire to see the devastated areas in all countries, in the Soviet Union, in Great Britain, in France, and elsewhere, restored, he felt that reparations could not possibly cover the needs. He concluded that he was in favor of extracting the maximum in reparations from Germany but not to the extent that the people would starve.

MR. MAISKY then stated that while he appreciated the Prime Minister's points concerning the experiences after the last war in the matter of reparations. he felt that the failure in this respect had been due not to the fact that the reparations had been too heavy but to the transfer problem which was the rock on which the reparations policy was founded. He said that he must add that the financial policies of the United States and Great Britain contributed to the German refusal to pay. He said that the Germans had never paid more than one-quarter of the total reparations figure and had received a great deal more in credits and loans. Mr. Maisky stated that the purpose of reparations in kind was to avoid the problem of transfer. He pointed out that the amount desired by the Soviet Union was equal only to 10% of the present United States budget and equal to about six months' of the British expenditures in the war. The Soviet demands for German reparations equaled about 1½ times the United States budget in peace and about 2½ times the British budget. He said, of course, there was no intention to force Germany into starvation but he pointed out that he did not feel that the Germans had a right to a higher standard of living than that of Central Europe. He said Germany can develop her light industry and agriculture and that since the Germans would have no military expenditures there was no reason why Germany could not give a modest but decent standard of living to her people. . . .

34

The Big Three at Yalta: The Private Agreement

This and Document 35 are the agreements on Germany reached at the Yalta meeting of the Big Three. This document was kept secret until the Cold War had developed, while Document 35 was released to the press immediately after the conclusion of the Yalta Conference. A quick comparison of the two makes evident the reason for the different treatment. The first included specific commitments to high reparations while the latter was phrased in the vague language to which diplomats are addicted.

Document†

III. Dismemberment of Germany

It was agreed that Article 12 (*a*) of the Surrender Terms for Germany should be amended to read as follows:

"The United Kingdom, the United States of America and the Union of Soviet Socialist Republics shall possess supreme authority with respect to Germany. In the exercise of such authority they will take such steps, including the complete disarmament, demilitarisation and the dismemberment of Germany as they deem requisite for future peace and security."

The study of the procedure for the dismemberment of Germany was referred to a Committee, consisting of Mr. Eden (Chairman), Mr. Winant and Mr. Gousev. This body would consider the desirability of associating with it a French representative.

IV. Zone of Occupation for the French and Control Council for Germany

It was agreed that a zone in Germany, to be occupied by the French Forces, should be allocated to France. This zone would be formed out of the British and American zones and its extent would be settled by the British and Americans in consultation with the French Provisional Government.

It was also agreed that the French Provisional Government should be invited to become a member of the Allied Control Council for Germany.

†From: Protocol of the Proceedings of the Crimea Conference, February 11, 1945, in U.S., Department of State, *FRUS, Yalta*, pp. 978-79.

V. Reparation

The following protocol has been approved:

1. Germany must pay in kind for the losses caused by her to the Allied nations in the course of the war. Reparations are to be received in the first instance by those countries which have borne the main burden of the war, have suffered the heaviest losses and have organised victory over the enemy.

2. Reparation in kind is to be exacted from Germany in three following forms:

a) Removals within 2 years from the surrender of Germany or the cessation of organised resistance from the national wealth of Germany located on the territory of Germany herself as well as outside her territory (equipment, machine-tools, ships, tolling stock, German investments abroad, shares of industrial, transport and other enterprises in Germany etc.), these removals to be carried out chiefly for purpose of destroying the war potential of Germany.

b) Annual deliveries of goods from current production for a period to be fixed.

c) Use of German labour.

3. For the working out on the above principles of a detailed plan for exaction of reparation from Germany an Allied Reparation Commission will be set up in Moscow. It will consist of three representatives—one from the Union of Soviet Socialist Republics, one from the United Kingdom and one from the United States of America.

4. With regard to the fixing of the total sum of the reparation as well as the distribution of it among the countries which suffered from the German aggression the Soviet and American delegations agreed as follows:

"The Moscow Reparation Commission should take in its initial studies as a basis for discussion the suggestion of the Soviet Government that the total sum of the reparation in accordance with the points (*a*) and (*b*) of the paragraph 2 should be 20 billion dollars and that 50% of it should go to the Union of Soviet Socialist Republics."

The British delegation was of the opinion that pending consideration of the reparation question by the Moscow Reparation Commission no figures of reparation should be mentioned.

The above Soviet-American proposal has been passed to the Moscow Reparation Commission as one of the proposals to be considered by the Commission. . . .

35

The Big Three at Yalta: The Public Agreement

Document†

The Occupation and Control of Germany

We have agreed on common policies and plans for enforcing the unconditional surrender terms which we shall impose together on Nazi Germany after German armed resistance has been finally crushed. These terms will not be made known until the final defeat of Germany has been accomplished. Under the agreed plan, the forces of the Three Powers will each occupy a separate zone of Germany. Coordinated administration and control has been provided for under the plan through a central Control Commission consisting of the Supreme Commanders of the Three Powers with headquarters in Berlin. It has been agreed that France should be invited by the Three Powers, if she should so desire, to take over a zone of occupation, and to participate as a fourth member of the Control Commission. The limits of the French zone will be agreed by the four governments concerned through their representatives on the European Advisory Commission.

It is our inflexible purpose to destroy German militarism and Nazism and to ensure that Germany will never again be able to disturb the peace of the world. We are determined to disarm and disband all German armed forces; break up for all time the German General Staff that has repeatedly contrived the resurgence of German militarism; remove or destroy all German military equipment; eliminate or control all German industry that could be used for military production; bring all war criminals to just and swift punishment and exact reparation in kind for the destruction wrought by the Germans; wipe out the Nazi party, Nazi laws, organizations and institutions, remove all Nazi and militarist influences from public office and from the cultural and economic life of the German people; and take in harmony such other measures in Germany as may be necessary to the future peace and safety of the world. It is not our purpose to destroy the people of Germany, but only when Nazism and Militarism have been extirpated will there be hope for a decent life for Germans, and a place for them in the comity of nations.

†From: Report of the Crimea Conference, February 11, 1945, in U.S., Department of State, *FRUS, Yalta*, pp. 970-71.

III. Reparation by Germany

We have considered the question of the damage caused by Germany to the Allied Nations in this war and recognized it as just that Germany be obliged to make compensation for this damage in kind to the greatest extent possible. A Commission for the Compensation of Damage will be established. The Commission will be instructed to consider the question of the extent and methods for compensating damage caused by Germany to the Allied Countries. The Commission will work in Moscow. . . .

36

"The Germans Cannot Escape Responsibility..."

By approving this memorandum, Roosevelt repudiated a State Department memo he had approved only a few weeks earlier. Even though Morgenthau considered that a small victory, this policy statement reflected the War Department's views and was a far cry from the Quebec memorandum initialed only seven months earlier.

Document†

[Annex]
Memorandum Regarding American Policy for the Treatment of Germany
[Washington,] March 23, 1945.

The following is a summary of U.S. policy relating to Germany in the initial post-defeat period. As such it will be introduced into the European Advisory Commission, and will be used as the basis for directives to be issued to the U.S. Commanding General in Germany.

The authority of the Control Council to formulate policy with respect to matters affecting Germany as a whole shall be paramount, and its agreed policies shall be carried out in each zone by the zone commander. In the absence of such agreed policies, and in matters exclusively affecting his own zone, the zone commander will exercise his authority in accordance with directives received from his own government.

The administration of affairs in Germany should be directed toward the decentralization of the political structure and the development of local responsibility. The German economy shall also be decentralized, except that to the minimum extent required for carrying out the purposes set forth herein, the Control Council may permit or establish central control of (a) essential national public services such as railroads, communications and power: (b) finance and foreign affairs, and (c) production and distribution of essential commodities. There shall be equitable distribution of such commodities between the several zones.

Germany's ruthless warfare and fanatical Nazi resistance have destroyed German economy and made chaos and suffering inevitable. The Germans cannot escape responsibility for what they have brought upon themselves.

†From: Memorandum Regarding American Policy for the Treatment of Germany, Annex to a memorandum from Joseph Grew to Roosevelt, March 23, 1945, in U.S., Department of State, *FRUS, 1945*, (Washington, D.C.: Government Printing Office, 1968), vol. 3, pp. 471-73.

Controls may be imposed upon the German economy only as may be necessary (a) to carry out programs of industrial disarmament and demilitarization, reparations, and of relief for liberated areas as prescribed by appropriate higher authority and (b) to assure the production and maintenance of goods and services required to meet the needs of the occupying forces and displaced persons in Germany, and essential to prevent starvation or such disease or civil unrest as would endanger the occupying forces. No action shall be taken, in execution of the reparations program or otherwise, which would tend to support basic living standards in Germany on a higher level than that existing in any one of the neighboring United Nations. All economic and financial international transactions, including exports and imports, shall be controlled with the aim of preventing Germany from developing a war potential and of achieving the other objectives named herein. The first charge on all approved exports for reparations or otherwise shall be a sum necessary to pay for imports. No extension of credit to Germany or Germans by any foreign person or Government shall be permitted, except that the Control Council may in special emergencies grant such permission. Recurrent reparations should not, by their form or amount, require the rehabilitation or development of German heavy industry and should not foster the dependence of other countries upon the German economy.

In the imposition and maintenance of economic controls. German authorities will to the fullest extent practicable be ordered to proclaim and assume administration of such controls. Thus it should be brought home to the German people that the responsibility for the administration of such controls and for any breakdowns in those controls, will rest with themselves and their own authorities.

The Nazi party and its affiliated and suprevised organizations and all Nazi public institutions shall be dissolved and their revival prevented. Nazi and militaristic activity or propaganda in any form shall be prevented.

There shall be established a coordinated system of control over German education designed completely to eliminate Nazi and militarist doctrines and to make possible the development of democratic ideas.

Nazi laws which provide the basis of the Hitler regime or which establish discriminations on grounds of race, creed or political opinion, shall be abolished.

All members of the Nazi party who have been more than nominal participants in its activities, and all other persons hostile to Allied purposes will be removed from public office and from positions of responsibility in private enterprise.

War criminals and those who have participated in planning or carrying out Nazi enterprises involving or resulting in atrocities or war crimes, shall be arrested, brought to trial and punished. Nazi leaders and influential Nazi supporters and any other persons dangerous to the occupation or its objectives, shall be arrested and interned.

A suitable program for the restitution of property looted by Germans shall be carried out promptly.

The German armed forces, including the General Staff, and all para-military organizations, shall be promptly demobilized and disbanded in such a manner as permanently to prevent their revival or reorganization.

The German war potential shall be destroyed. As part of the program to attain this objective, all implements of war and all specialized facilities for the production of armaments shall be seized or destroyed. The maintenance and production of all aircraft and implements of war shall be prevented.

Joseph C. Grew	Frank Coe
J.H. Hilldring	Harry D. White
H. Freeman Matthews	William L. Clayton
John J. McCloy	Henry Morgenthau, Jr.

37 ═══════════

═══════════ The Military
Decision:
Against
Deindustrial-
ization

The connection between military strategy and politics may sometimes be
hidden, but not for long. As Morgenthau had long feared, political
considerations would eventually predominate, and this cable from General
Marshall to General Eisenhower proves the point. Eisenhower responded that
he also hoped that the military occupation of the Ruhr could take place with
a minimum of destruction of industrial facilities.

Document†
FROM: AGWAR, FROM GENERAL MARSHALL
  TO: SHAEF FORWARD, FOR GENERAL EISENHOWER FOR HIS
       EYES ONLY
REF NO: W-64236, 6 April 1945

Discussion here by G-2 and Mr. STIMSON relates to effect of complete
destruction of RUHR industry on economic future of EUROPE, destruction
that would result from further Allied offensive action. Admiral LEAHY,
KING, HANDY and HULL are opposed to asking you any question.

Aside from purely military considerations concerned with advancement of
campaign to destroy the German Army there are two schools of thought in
high government circles here regarding a post war pastoral GERMANY and a
policy of leaving some industrial capability to benefit the related economy of
other European countries lacking RUHR resources.

We naturally assume that you are proceeding in the manner best adapted
to the security and rapidity of your thrusts into GERMANY.

Without thought of compromising yourself or in effect limiting your
present military intentions will you please give me for no other eyes but Mr.
STIMSON's, mine, HANDY's and HULL's, most confidentially your present
intentions as to RUHR pocket and your view as to desirability or feasibility
of any procedure by which the RUHR proper might be sealed off.

I assume your forces are already deeply committed to operations directed
against the pocket. This message must not in any way embarrass you or have

†From: Marshall to Eisenhower, April 6. 1945, Eisenhower Papers, Dwight D.
Eisenhower Library, Abilene, Kansas.

the slightest effect in limiting your present point of view or intentions. As yet I have no views whatsoever in this matter, except that I think the fat is probably now in the fire and whatever the political conclusions it is too late, to[o] impracticable to take any action for such reason.

38

The Military Decision: For Reconstruction

The following excerpts from two letters sent by General Lucius D. Clay to Secretary of State James F. Byrnes and Assistant Secretary of War John McCloy provide ample evidence of his belief that Germany had already suffered enough destruction through warfare. Clay obviously believed that Germany had to be reconstructed and he used the vagueness in JCS 1067 to implement his views.

Document†

Conditions in Germany are getting progressively worse and large sections of all important cities have been obliterated. Of course, we have a long range problem in preventing the restoration of Germany's war potential. However, this is not the short range problem as several years will be required to develop even a sustaining economy to provide a bare minimum standard of living. The coming winter months will be most difficult.

I think that too much of our planning at home has envisaged a Germany in which an existing government has surrendered with a large part of the country intact. In point of fact, it looks as if every foot of ground will have to be occupied. Destruction will be widespread, and government as we know it will be non-existent. In solving the short range problem we should find the answer to the long range problem, if at the same time we develop unanimity of action among the Allies.

Document††

I think that Washington must revise its thinking relative to destruction of Germany's war potential as an immediate problem. The progress of war has accomplished that and it is in view now (based on general impressions, I must admit) that the industry which remains, with few exceptions, even when restored will suffice barely for a very long minimum living standard in Germany.

If this is to be provided, we must have sufficient freedom here to bring industries back into production for that purpose. To accomplish this will

†From: Clay to Byrnes, April 20, 1945, in *The Papers of General Lucius D. Clay; Germany, 1945-1949,* ed. Jean Edward Smith, 2 vols. Bloomington: Indiana University Press, 1974), vol. 1, p. 6.

††From: Clay to McCloy, April 26, 1945, in *The Papers of General Lucius D. Clay,* vol. 1, p. 8.

require production controls. They cannot be avoided if we are to succeed in establishing reasonable order and meet essential needs of the occupying forces. I hope our final directive will not prohibit us from establishing such controls as are needed.

Similarly, we should not be too hasty in listing specific reparations. They, too, could make it impossible to bring order back into Germany.

I hope you won't think from the above that I am getting soft. I realize the necessity for stern and spartan treatment. However, retribution now is far greater than realized at home and our planes and artillery have really carried war direct to the homes of the German people.

It is going to take all we can do to re-establish government services and a semblance of national economy for many months. This much must be done if only to make it possible to govern Germany with comparatively small occupational forces.

When it has been done, we can look at the long range picture with more clarity and understanding. Certainly, if the Allies intend to enforce compliance with their terms over the years, they can well make the decisions as to what to destroy after the facts have been gathered, rather than in haste based on data which war has rendered valueless.

39

"Being 'Hard' on Germany Does Not Call for Unnecessary Destruction"

In this letter to the director of the War Department's Civil Affairs Division, Clay outlined his desire for full discretionary authority and a more positive policy aimed at redeveloping the German economy. His harsh words for Bernard Bernstein came because the colonel, former aide to Morgenthau, continued to support an occupation policy, modeled on The Morgenthau Plan.

Document†

I doubt if Colonel [Bernard] Bernstein is big enough to handle the overall financial problem. He is very smart and energetic but is somewhat warped in his judgment of the problem as a whole. In this field we need a really big man. We also need several outstanding economists, able to view the picture as a whole and develop long-range programs. They can do little in helping us evolve our short-range programs but are needed in developing a long-range philosophy.

I am somewhat disturbed over rumors which we get with respect to various commissions being set up. Of course, the Reparations Commission was set up at Yalta. Since then we understand here that consideration is being given to separate Commissions for Restitutions for the Trial of War Criminals, for the Internationalization of the Ruhr and for other purposes. We are going to face many difficulties in making the Allied Control Authority work. To me it seems clear that if it doesn't work we might as well throw the idea of a United Nations out of the window. If it is to work, the representative governments must be willing to place responsibility in their representatives on the Group Council and to give them enough authority to carry out its responsibilities. The more additional commissions that are created, the more places we have to develop discord and the less chance we have to make a successful experiment out of our proposed controls for Germany. Of course,

†From: Clay to General John Hilldring, May 7, 1945, in *The Papers of General Lucius D. Clay*, pp. 12, 13.

this argument sounds like the usual argument profered by the bureaucrat who wants to create and preserve for himself his own independent empire. The only evidence to the contrary that we will ever be able to present will be our showing that we are trying to develop a framework to pass over to the appropriate civil agency at an early date. If that framework is to be sound it must be the framework of government in Germany and the American representatives must in fact truly represent the United States in Germany. If the Reparations Commission in Moscow limits itself to policy we can still develop satisfactory working arrangements. However, if it is to specify item and quantity, then it, and not the Allied Control Authority, will actually write the ticket for the German economy.

I hope that this letter does not sound pessimistic. I am an optimist at heart and still have faith that the Allied Control Authority can and will work. If it does it will be because the representatives of each government have sufficient discretionary authority to give and take in conference and to develop harmony through compromise. To me, being "hard" on Germany does not call for unnecessary destruction of economy. It can be accomplished over a long period of time only if we permit Germany a reasonably decent standard of living under controls which prevent the direction and expansion of those types and kinds of industry which are adaptable to war purposes. Being "hard" now is important psychologically to show the German people how badly German military might has been defeated. However, that is really easy to do compared with establishing controls which will require firm agreement among the Nations and a determination to continue the control of Germany for many years.

40

The End of the Morgenthau Plan, March, 1946

To Lucius Clay, there were only two choices for Germany; communism or American-style democracy and economics. Like most Americans, he believed communism could appeal only to those with empty stomachs and supported the idea of food as a political weapon. Whatever remnants of the Morgenthau Plan might have existed in the late 1940s quickly disappeared under the pressure of Cold War. Among the casualties was the idea of a neutral, disengaged Germany.

Document†

.....It is our belief that the Russian zone is feeding approximately 1500 calories and will continue to do so until the next harvest season.

We have insisted on democratic processes in the U.S. zone and have maintained a strict neutrality between political parties. As a result the Communist Party has made little inroad. However, there is no choice between becoming a Communist on 1500 calories and a believer in democracy on 1000 calories. It is my sincere belief that our proposed ration allowance in Germany will not only defeat our objectives in middle Europe but will pave the road to a Communist Germany.

I know of no additional data which we can furnish you which has not been furnished. As the occupying power in our own zone we have assumed some obligations even though the Germans are an enemy people. It would seem to me that we are making the accomplishment of our objectives impossible....

†From: Clay to Echols and Peterson, March 27, 1946, in *The Papers of General Lucius Clay*, vol. p, p. 184.

part three

Bibliographic Essay

The basic story surrounding the Morgenthau Plan for Germany can be found in two documentary collections: U.S. Department of State, *Foreign Relations of the United States (FRUS)* (Washington, D.C.: Government Printing Office, 1862-), particularly the volume titled *Conference at Quebec, 1944* published in 1972; and U.S., Congress, Senate, Subcommittee to Investigate the Administration of the Internal Security Act and Other Internal Security Laws of the Committee on the Judiciary, 90th Cong., 1st sess., *Morgenthau Diary (Germany)* 2 vols. (Washington, D.C.: Government Printing Office, 1967). Valuable additional materials can be found in the State Department Archives in the National Archives in Washington, D.C., in the Roosevelt papers and the Morgenthau diary/papers at the Franklin D. Roosevelt Library in Hyde Park, N.Y., and in the Prime Minister's Operational and Confidential papers (Premier 3 and 4) and Foreign Office papers (FO 371) at the Public Record Office in London, England. Insights into Russian policy can be found in Ministry of Foreign Affairs of the USSR, *Stalin's Correspondence with Roosevelt and Truman, and Churchill and Atlee, 1941-1945* (New York: Capricorn Books, 1965), although those documents give no indication of Stalin's original desire for a harsh peace and the permanent division of Germany—a choice of documents which reflects Cold War needs. A recently published and illuminating collection of documents which relate to the actual occupation of Germany is Jean Edward Smith ed., *The Papers of General Lucius D. Clay: Germany, 1945-1949*, 2 vols. Bloomington: Indiana Univ. Press, 1974). Henry Morgenthau, Jr. published a comprehensive defense of his plan titled *Germany is Our Problem* (New York: Harper & Brothers, 1945).

A number of memoirs, when used with proper caution, afford real insights into the policy debate over Germany in general and the Morgenthau Plan in particular. The most useful, in spite of a remarkable lack of self-doubt, is Henry Stimson and McGeorge Bundy, *On Active Service in Peace and War* (New York: Harper & Brothers, 1948). John Morton Blum's quasi-memoir, *From the Morgenthau Diaries: Years of War, 1941-1945* (Boston: Houghton Mifflin, 1967) utilized other secondary sources for background material, but is essentially written from Morgenthau's point of view. It must, however, be supplemented by research in the Morgenthau diaries themselves, particularly the so-called Presidential Diary in which Morgenthau recorded his notes on conversations with President Roosevelt. The best insight into Churchill's thinking about Germany and the Morgenthau plan comes from Lord Moran, *Churchill, Taken From the Diaries of Lord Moran: The Struggle for Survival, 1940-1965* (Boston: Houghton Mifflin, 1966). Churchill's own memoirs touch on the Morgenthau Plan and planning for Germany, but with misleading brevity. See Winston S. Churchill, *The Second World War*, 6 vols. (Boston: Houghton Mifflin, 1948-1953), especially the last three volumes. *The Memoirs of Anthony Eden* (Earl of Avon), vol. 2, *The Reckoning* (Boston: Houghton Mifflin, 1965) do not indicate Eden's ambiguous attitude toward Germany, but occasionally adds information not otherwise available. Robert Sherwood's study of *Roosevelt and Hopkins* (New York: Harper & Brothers, 1950), another quasi-memoir, is based too extensively on the Hopkins papers and Sherwood's personal recollections as a Roosevelt speechwriter to be completely reliable, though it adds much color and human interest. The memoirs by James F. Byrnes, *Speaking Frankly* (New York: Harper & Brothers, 1947), Dean Acheson, *Present at the Creation* (New York: W.W. Norton, 1969), Lucius D. Clay, *Decision in Germany* (Garden City, N.Y.: Doubleday & Co., 1950), and Ivan Maisky, *Memoirs of a Soviet Ambassador: The War, 1939-1943*, Andrew Rothstein, trans. (London: Hutchinson & Co., 1967) are all largely peripheral to the time frame of this study, though each contributed background material and perspective. *The Memoirs of Cordell Hull*, 2 vols. (London: Hodder & Stoughton, 1948) are probably the most factually unrealiable of all World War II memoirs, although they provide an accurate picture of how Hull thought history ought to have happened.

A few volumes from the various official histories of World War II include material related to the Morgenthau Plan. Forrest C. Pogue's *The Supreme Command* (Washington, D.C.: Government Printing Office, 1954) remains the best analysis of SHAEF and its commander, General Eisenhower; and Maurice Matloff's *Strategic Planning for Coalition Warfare, 1943-1944* (Washington, D.C.: Government Printing Office, 1959) is useful for any examination of the Combined Chiefs of Staff. Both are volumes in the series *United States Army in World War* published by the Office of the Chief of Military History. Sir Llewellyn Woodward's *British Foreign Policy in the Second World War* comes in two versions: an abridged volume (London: HMSO, 1962), and three volumes completed to date of a projected four or five volume series (London: HMSO, 1970-   ). Unfortunately, most of the story of British planning for postwar Germany will be in the volumes not yet published, so scholars must presently use the abridged version. The books are seemingly an attempt merely to recreate the facts as they happened, but a look at the unpublished documents makes it clear that Woodward, like every other historian, selected his evidence in accordance with his prejudices. Two other useful volumes in the British official history are John Ehrman, *Grand Strategy*, vols. 5 and 6 (London: HMSO¸ 1956). Harley Notter, *Postwar Foreign Policy Preparation* (Washington, D.C.: Government Printing Office, 1949) is a bland but informative combination memoir/official history by a State Department official.

There are only two in-depth and up to date scholarly studies of American planning for postwar Germany. Paul Y. Hammond, "Directives for the Occupation of Germany: The Washington Controversy," in *American Civil-Military Decisions*, ed, Harold Stein (Birmingham: Univ. of Alabama Press, 1963), pp. 311-460 examines bureaucratic planning in great detail. Hammond incorporates the material from two books by participants; Harold Zink, *The United States in Germany, 1944-1955* (Princeton, N.J.: D. Van Nostrand, 1957) and Hajo Hoborn, *American Military Government* (Washington: Infantry Journal Press, 1947), though both add some detail, particularly regarding War Department actions. Bruce Kuklick, *American Policy and the Division of Germany: The Clash with Russia over Reparations* (Ithaca,N.Y.: Cornell Univ. Press, 1972) is primarily interested in the reparations question, since he believes that it was the problem which determined Germany's fate. Nevertheless, he provides detailed background on other questions, including the Morgenthau Plan. More important, his analysis of the inertial force behind the State Department's liberal capitalism (multilateralism, as he calls it) is critical to any understanding of American foreign policy during World War II—even if one disagrees as to the degree of concensus those policies commanded. There are a number of articles written in the 1950s and 1960s which deal with the Morgenthau Plan and which Kuklick cites in his bibliography. Both he and Hammond have made excellent use of those articles (some of which were written by participants) and there is little need to cite them here. The same is true for the long list of journalistic accounts published immediately following the war.

Some other secondary accounts represent the latest scholarship on the German question. William M. Franklin, "Zonal Boundaries and Access to Berlin," *World Politics*, vol. 16 (October, 1963), pp. 1-36, appears to be the definitive treatment of the question of zonal boundaries, although it does not explain Roosevelt's decision to accept the southern zone in Germany. The question of American policy and the Soviet Union as a factor in postwar planning for Germany is illuminated by George C. Herring, "Lend-Lease to Russia and the Origins of the Cold War, 1944-1945," *Journal of American History*, vol. 61 (June, 1969), pp. 93-114, and his book, *Aid to Russia, 1941-1946* (New York: Columbia Univ. Press, 1973) plus Thomas G.

Paterson's "The Abortive American Loan to Russia and the Origins to the Cold War, 1943-1946," *Journal of American History*, vol. 611 (June, 1969), pp. 70-92, and his book, *Soviet-American Confrontation: Postwar Reconstruction and the Origins of the Cold War* (Baltimore: Johns Hopkins Univ. Press, 1973). The problem of France as a factor in the early days of the American occupation of Germany is discussed in Lloyd C. Gardner, *Architects of Illusion: Men and Ideas in American Foreign Policy, 1941-1949* (Chicago: Quadrangle Books, 1970), and John Gimbel, *The American Occupation of Germany: Politics and the Military, 1945-1949* (Stanford: Stanford Univ. Press, 1968). Gimbel, in a limited way, criticizes Gardner's thesis that militant German socialism and Russo-American confrontation were the key problems in Germany in a review essay, "Cold War: German Front," *The Maryland Historian*, vol. 2 (Spring, 1971), pp. 41-55. All of these studies, regardless of their differences, treat the German question as one which was resolved, not by Roosevelt's death, but by decisions made by Truman in the postwar years.

A number of general studies of World War II diplomacy provide indispensable background material for any study of a specific problem. John Gaddis, *The United States and the Origins of the Cold War, 1941-1947* (New York: Columbia Univ. Press, 1972) is a good overview, though it must be supplemented by additional documentary research for individual episodes. Gabriel Kolko, *The Politics of War* (New York: Random House, 1968) posits a totally depersonalized concept of history. Following the general thesis that all American policy-makers held the same views and therefore saw the Soviet Union as a threat, Kolko argues that Morgenthau and Harry White constructed the Morgenthau Plan as part of an overall plot to prevent the Russians from getting extensive reparations. The opposite extreme is taken by Anthony Kubek in "The Evolution of the 'Treasury Plan' for Postwar Germany: An Introduction to the Morgenthau Diary on Germany," in *Morgenthau Diary (Germany)*, cited above, Kubek argues that the Morgenthau Plan was a plot hatched in Moscow and implemented by such communist agents in the Treasury Department as Harry White. As ever with World War II diplomacy, William H. McNeill, *America, Britain, & Russia: Their Co-Operation and Conflict, 1941-1946* (London: Oxford Univ. Press, 1953), provides insights and historical context, while Herbert Feis, *Churchill, Roosevelt, Stalin* (Princeton, N.J.: Princeton Univ. Press, 1957) does likewise, though it tends to concentrate too much on only the Big Three leaders. Feis adds additional detail and much more interpretation and opinion on the German question in *From Trust to Terror: The Onset of the Cold War, 1945-1950* (New York: W.W. Norton, 1970). Details on the most controversial of the World War II summit meetings is found in Diane S. Clemens, *Yalta* (New York: Oxford Univ. Press, 1970). One of the latest pieces of British scholarship on World War II diplomacy, John W. Wheeler-Bennett and Anthony Nicholls, *The Semblance of Peace: The Political Settlement After the Second World War* (London: Macmillan, 1972), reflects a very strong belief that Russian intransigence and American naivete brought on the Cold War. Raymond G. O'Connor's *Diplomacy for Victory: FDR and Unconditional Surrender* (New York: W.W. Norton, 1971) is persuasive, readable, and far broader than its title indicates. Elting E. Morison's biography for Henry L. Stimson, *Turmoil and Tradition* (Boston: Houghton Mifflin, 1960) provides an excellent summary of Stimson's proposals for postwar Germany and, more importantly, places them within context of Stimson's overall political philosophy and moral code. The only recent dissertation which is devoted to a study of the Morgenthau Plan is an overly long and tendentious one based on printed sources; Meredith L. Adams, "The Morgenthau Plan: A Study in Bureaucratic Depravity" (Univ. of Texas, 1971).

The relationship between military operations and planning for Germany can be traced through the books by Pogue and Matloff cited above, although Forrest Pogue's *George C. Marshall: Organizer of Victory, 1943-1945* (New York: The Viking Press, 1973) adds so much detail and new information that it is indispensable for any person endeavoring to understand the relationship between politics and military strategy during World War II. Stephen E. Ambrose, *Eisenhower and Berlin: The Decision to Halt at the Elbe* (New York: W.W. Norton, 1967) effectively argues that the decision was strictly based upon military considerations. The late Cornelius Ryan has rescued the battle of Arnhem from undeserved oblivion in a journalistic account, *A Bridge Too Far* (New York: Simon and Schuster, 1974).

The foreign policy of Stalin and the Soviet Union can be partly traced through *Stalin's Correspondence* and the Anglo-American documents and memoirs, all cited above. Adam Ulam's speculations in *Expansion and Coexistence: The History of Soviet Foreign Policy, 1917-1967* (New York: Frederick A. Praeger, 1968) demonstrate both the strengths and limitations of such research restrictions.

Although this bibliography is obviously not designed as a guide for researchers, it will provide direction for those who wish to read more about the question of postwar planning for Germany during World War II. Those who wish to do additional research should, after examining the documents, consult the specialized bibliographies and citations in the books by Kuklick, Gimbel, Kolko, and Pogue which are cited above.